RURAL MARKETING
Targeting the Non-urban Consumer

SANAL KUMAR VELAYUDHAN

Response Books
A division of Sage Publications
New Delhi • Thousand Oaks • London

First published in 2002 by

Response Books
A division of Sage Publications India Pvt Ltd
M–32, Greater Kailash Market–I, New Delhi 110 048

Sage Publications Inc.   Sage Publications Ltd
2455 Teller Road   6 Bonhill Street
Thousand Oaks, California 91320   London EC2A 4PU

Published by Tejeshwar Singh for Response Books, typeset in 11.5 pt. Sanskrit-New Caledonia by S.R. Enterprises, New Delhi, and printed at Chaman Offset Printers, New Delhi.

Library of Congress Cataloging-in-Publication Data

Velayudhan, Sanal Kumar, 1955-
   Rural marketing: targeting the non-urban consumer/Sanal Kumar
   Velayudhan.
      p.cm.
   Includes bibliographical references (p.).
   1. Marketing—India. 2. Consumer behavior—India. 3. India—Rural
   conditions. I. Title.
   HF5415.12.15 V45 2002   658.8'7'00954091734—dc21   2001048723

ISBN: 0-7619-9565-X (US-HB)   81-7829-050-2 (India-HB)
   0-7619-9566-8 (US-PB)   81-7829-051-0 (India-PB)

Production Team: Leela Gupta, R.A.M. Brown and Santosh Rawat

Fondly dedicated to:

My parents, **Rajamma Nair** and **Neilakanta Velayudhan Nair**
For educating me on the social processes
and
Devika *and* ***Akshaya***
Who gave me enough reasons to re-examine the social processes

Contents

Contents

List of Tables

List of Figures

Preface

The discovery of an eighth of the world's population as potential consumers by the organised sector is a recent one. With such a large untapped market potential, the rural marketer would wonder at the purpose of this book. The main objective is to provide guidelines for decision making in rural markets by:

- Highlighting critical issues in rural markets;
- Providing options for marketers;
- Developing insights into the behaviour of the rural consumer;
- Understanding rural institutions of retailers, *haats* and *melas* (rural markets and fairs); and
- Addressing these issues using insights into consumer behaviour and rural institutions.

The rural marketer is faced with an entirely different set of conditions when marketing in rural areas as compared to urban areas. Managing a rural market environment becomes difficult because of the:

- Limited literature and absence of a framework to guide decision making in rural markets; and
- Culture variations that require not only new methods, but also unlearning old ones, and attitude changes.

These problems are compounded by the logistics which form a barrier to the rural market. The 'not-for-us' philosophy and the attitude of 'we tried, but it is not worth the effort', thus finds favour in the face of these challenges. Pioneers in the rural market command consumer loyalty and retail shelf space. Discovering the distant market early is therefore critical. The marketer cannot afford to wait, hoping to tap the potential at some later date. Entrenched competition will make entry into rural markets at a later point very difficult.

An organised framework that understands these markets is needed to guide decision making. I realised this when I was working on an assignment for 'village adoption' as early as the late seventies. While researching the market for credit, we faced problems in methodology and implementation. One amusing situation we faced was that questions to a respondent brought responses from any one of the many other people surrounding us in the group. The difference in consumer behaviour therefore affects not only marketing to the rural consumer but also researching the rural consumer. The use of standard research methodologies has only limited relevance. The effort to understand this market has been, and is, a continuing pursuit. In 1993, while at XLRI, Jamshedpur, I launched the first Management Development Programme on 'Rural Marketing'. The programme continued for three years till I left XLRI in 1997. I then joined the Administrative Staff College of India (ASCI), but did not relaunch this programme till 1999. Today, the programme designed by me at ASCI is not the same as the one in operation in 1993.

The rural market environment has changed between 1993 and 1999. The issues in 1993 were simpler, but today with the novelty value of products gone, rural markets stubbornly refuse to take just any product and service created for urban markets. Understanding rural consumers and using the appropriate research approach to these markets has become as important as the logistics of rural marketing. The need for a systematic approach to rural marketing is keenly felt. My book is an effort to bridge this gap. It draws on my work in this field and the interaction with marketers serving the rural consumers. I expect this book to start as well as strengthen the process of conceptualising and developing the framework for rural marketing.

The book was conceived and produced over the past year and a half, but the concepts, short cases and information have been accumulated over a number of years. I wish to thank several individuals and organisations who have made this book possible. The participants in the programme on Rural Marketing, both at XLRI, Jamshedpur and at ASCI, have contributed valuable insights. The questioning minds of the post graduate students in Business Management at XLRI were also of enormous help.

Research work carried out on behalf of many organisations was a rich source of information. Many persons in these organisations contributed to the work. Special mention must be made of C. Paul Francis, Sitaram Textiles, P. Srinivas, Uttam Beedis, Radhe Shyam of Crane Supari, Raju of Milma, S. Venkatesan, Ministry of Personnel & Training, Government of India, Verghese Mathew, K.S.O.

Finally, my special thanks to Komala Raj for her help in typing several drafts of the book before it took this final shape.

Sanal Kumar Velayudhan

ONE

Rural Marketing: Opportunities and Challenges

This chapter captures situations that reflect the growing interest and enthusiasm of business towards rural markets. Opportunities in the rural market are examined in light of intense and growing competition in urban markets. The market opportunities are clearly perceived through a comparison of consumption patterns for durables as well as non-durables between the rural and urban markets. Identifying opportunities and clarity in decision making requires an unambiguous definition of rural marketing. Rural marketing and rural markets are conceptualised to clearly distinguish them from urban marketing and urban markets.

The Road Map

India's vast rural market offers a huge potential for a marketer facing stiff competition in the urban markets. The rural market environment is very different from the familiar surroundings of the urban market. Rural consumers have customs and behaviour that the marketer may find difficult to contend with.

The understanding of India's rural markets is an important objective of this book. The other major objective is to comprehend influences on this market. The emphasis is on understanding the consumer response to marketing decision variables. The third objective of the book is to develop appropriate methods to research rural markets.

This is important in the context of the rural market for two reasons: (*a*) the consumers' ability to discriminate varies; and (*b*) reference points used by the rural consumer differ from those of the urban consumers. The research methods to measure perception, attitudes and behaviour in rural markets vary from the approach used in researching urban markets. Research methods unsuitable in rural markets create a distorted picture of the consumer and results in failure of marketing efforts.

The opportunities in the rural market are demonstrated by comparing consumption levels in urban and rural markets for different product categories. Their volumes and growth show the importance of this market. Understanding demographic profiles of consumers and their response to brand offering is a useful approach to analyse the rural market. A large number of caselets in the book capture the consumer response to brand offering. The need for appropriate methodology for researching consumers is demonstrated by the non-applicability of the urban reference points and measures in the context of rural markets. Literature available on rural development provides alternative methods to research rural markets. The understanding of the rural consumer is utilised in decision-making situations. Organising the chapters according to 'marketing decision variables' provides the focus on 'decision making'. The critical aspect of reaching the consumer with the message and the product offered is examined in great detail. Short cases and data illustrated later in this book provide the decision maker with important criteria to evaluate options in these markets. The influence of consumer perceptions on product design in different product-market situations is identified. Consequently, the concepts and framework developed are relevant for marketing decisions.

The use of an existing network of channels in the rural market is the key to connecting with the rural heartland. *Haats* and *melas* that are unique to rural markets, supplement the retailer route to rural markets. The interaction between consumers and these unique institutions provide information for use in marketing decisions. The marketing strategy is examined in the context of the competitive situation in the rural market. Competition is categorised into (*a*) generic competition, (*b*) competition with the unorganised sector, (*c*) entry into the market and (*d*) meeting the challenges created by imitations. The challenges faced by the marketer in these competitive situations match the opportunities available in rural markets.

Corporate Interest in Rural Markets

When rural customers discover the new and exciting choice of brands available in urban markets, a demand for these brands is created in rural areas. When Titan found rural consumers purchasing their Sonata brand of quartz watches, they formulated a marketing strategy tailored to the requirements of the large rural market.

There is an increase in the launch of new products and brands in rural areas. In many product categories like cigarettes, biscuits or soaps, specific brands are developed for rural markets. The rural market, in both durables and non-durables, can be developed through new products and suitable positioning (see Box 1.1).

Box 1.1
Growing Importance of Rural Markets

- Hindustan Motors (HM) launched a utility vehicle the RTV (rural transport vehicle), aimed at the rural market. One way of meeting the intense competition in the passenger car segment by HM is through increased efforts in rural markets. It has over 40 percent of this rural market, exploiting the low prices, reliability and time tested rugged aspect of the Ambassador brand.

- Titan Industries, the country's largest watch-maker is now set to aggressively woo the rural consumer. Titan intends to make in-roads into the Indian hinterland with 'Sonata'. The company's watches are available in towns with a population of 20,000. Rural consumers who come to larger towns have access to Titan products. Titan now plans to have a specific product, specific communication and distribution for this market. It is now in the process of conducting research in rural markets. Titan's research in rural markets is mainly to find out how consumers perceive their product, their expectations on price or service and even on what they expect out of the watches. The main rural thrust is expected just before the wedding season of March–April of year 2001 (Rai, 2000).

Reasons for the Interest

There are quite a few reasons for the growing interest in rural markets. Their vast untapped potential, increasing income and purchasing power, improved accessibility and the increasing competition in urban markets make rural markets an attractive destination for jaded marketers of products and services.

Untapped Potential: Rural markets offer a great potential for marketing branded goods and services for two reasons:

- The large number of consumers. A pointer to this is the larger volume of sales of certain products in rural areas as compared to the sales of the same products in urban areas;
- Largely untapped markets. The penetration levels for many products are low in rural areas.

Market Size and Penetration: The estimated size of India's rural market stated as the percentage of world population is 12.2 percent. This means 12.2 percent of the world's consumers live in rural India. In numbers, this works out to about 120 million households. In India, the rural households form about 72 percent of the total households. This is a huge market by world standards.

Rural consumers own only 52 percent of available consumer durables, even though they form 72 percent of the total households in India. On an average rural households own three consumer durables as compared to seven consumer durables owned by an average urban household (NCAER, 1998). The gap clearly indicates the untapped potential among the large number of rural households.

Current Consumption a Pointer to Potential: The purchase and use of certain durables and non-durables by consumers in rural areas is more than that of consumers in urban areas.

The durables for which purchase and use by consumers in rural areas exceed those in urban areas are as follows (NCAER, 1998):

- Sewing machines;
- Radio/transistors;
- Wristwatches;
- Black and white television sets;
- Cassette recorders;
- Bicycles;

- Table fans;
- Pressure cookers.

In the case of consumer non-durables, there are at least six products where the rural market has a larger share than the urban market (see Table 1.1).

Table 1.1
Rural Market Share of Consumption

Non-durable Product	Share of Rural Percentage
Analgesic tablets	45.7
Batteries	56.2
Blues	52.3
Coconut oil	41.6
Iodised salt	51.4
Safety razor blades	54.1
Tea	51.3
Toilet soaps	41.9
Washing cakes/bars	54.6
Washing powders/liquids	46.4

Source: *Business World*, 7–21, April 1999.

Increasing Income and Purchasing Power

The agriculture development programmes of the government have helped to increase income in the agriculture sector. This in turn has created greater purchasing power in rural markets. Studies by the NCAER provide evidence of the increased income of rural households. Households in the lower income group have reduced while there is a strong growth in the number of households in upper middle and higher income households (see Table 1.2).

Rural Marketing: Opportunities and Challenges • 23

Table 1.2
Average Annual Growth Rates of Rural Households in Different Income Groups (figures are in percentages)

Income Group (Annual Income (Rs.) at 1995–96 prices	1985–86 to 1989–90	1992–93 to 1995–96
< 25,000 L	–0.20	–3.03
25,001–50,000 LM	4.91	10.22
50,001–77,000 M	17.82	3.11
77,001–1,06,000 WM	16.39	12.25
> 1,06,000 H	13.9	15.68
Total	2.04	1.44

Source: NCAER, 1998.

Accessibility of Markets

The attraction of a market depends not only on its potential but also on its accessibility. A market that cannot be exploited is a case of 'sour grapes'. Development of infrastructural facilities and marketing institutions have increased the accessibility of these markets

The road network has facilitated a systemised product distribution system to villages. In the past, companies relied on a 'trickle down' of stocks' to the buyer in interior villages that resulted from the active participation of channel members. In this system, the village retailer made fortnightly purchase visits to a bigger retailer in the nearest *tehsil* (sub-division of a district) level town. The large retailer in the *tehsil* town procures goods from the district headquarters. The district headquarters were therefore the terminal point of the company distribution channel. Today, an increasing number of companies are supplying village markets directly. Increasing direct contacts to villages helps product promotion and availability of the product in the village shop. Marketers of durable goods use direct contacts as a means to promote and attract rural consumers to dealer points in large feeder villages or towns.

Feeder villages or towns are locations from where a large number of interior villages get their products. Delivery-cum-promotion vans traversing eight to 10 villages a day and covering *haats* or *mandis* (markets), is the widely used method of direct contact in rural areas.

Competition in Urban Markets

Intensified competition in urban markets increases costs and reduces market share. The rural markets are therefore increasingly attractive in relation to urban markets. The automobile market brings this out clearly. Rajdoot motorcycles, Bajaj scooters or Ambassador cars find ready acceptance in rural markets as compared to urban markets where there is a proliferation of brands.

Consumer Behaviour Changes

Increased literacy and greater awareness in rural markets create new demands and discriminating buyers. This is observed more in the younger generation. In villages today, this segment of buyers consumes a large variety of products, both durables and non-durables. There is a visible increase in the consumption and use of a variety of products which is easily observed. The younger generation appears to seek variety and are more discriminating buyers. The young adult in a village likes to sport a fashionable watch. The preferred brand of toilet soap for the youth is not necessarily Lifebuoy, the brand preferred by the elders.

Box 1.2
Cellular Czars Rework Marketing Strategies

Cellular operators across the country are seeing more than 50 percent of all incremental growth in their cellular business coming from small towns and rural areas, not necessarily from mobile-totting rich farmers atop tractors.

Cellphones have reached the man on the cycle, the fisherman and the village *sarpanch* in the not-so-prosperous villages and towns in India. So much so, that some operators say they do not even need to explain in detail what a cellphone is—the villagers are already aware.

Out of the 5,40,000 total subscribers, BPL now has close to 2,00,000 subscribers in small markets across Maharashtra, Kerala and Tamil Nadu. Out of the 204 towns outside Mumbai that it has a presence in, 160 are small towns and villages. In Andhra Pradesh and Karnataka, Bharati now has about 30 percent of its total subscriber base in smaller towns and villages and the growth in these markets is much faster.

Marketing strategies are being reworked with plans for a lower tariff. 'Our average tariffs are lower in the smaller towns at Rs. 2.75 per minute as against Rs. 4 per minute in Delhi. This is possible because our investment in creating the infrastructure in smaller towns is far lower. "We are taking the Airtel brand to smaller markets through a multi-lingual advertising campaign"', says Anil Nair, head of Bharati's mobile operators across circles. Hutchison is trying to figure out how to expand the list of 1,850 villages and small towns where it currently offers cellular services. It too, is looking at introducing localised tariff structures (Law, 2000).

Organisations Rework Their Strategies for the Rural Markets

The peculiarities of rural markets have forced marketers to rework their marketing strategies developed for the urban markets. It is not only the product, but also the message, media, channel and prices that are tailored to meet the needs of the rural markets.

- Union Carbide has heavy brass torches for the rural markets instead of the slick plastic torches it has for the urban markets;

- Velvette shampoo was introduced in sachets and helped develop the rural market for shampoos as it was readily accepted;
- Castrol an engine oil brand has developed a movie with the lead characters having brand names and the message for the product woven into the story.

This approach reflects the recognition by marketers of the differing characteristics of the rural markets as opposed to urban markets. Rural markets are unique for the following reasons:

- The wants of rural consumers to meet a need is not necessarily the same as for urban consumers. These wants are shaped by a number of factors including the environment. The rural consumer who buys a vehicle for meeting his transportation need may want a rugged rather than a sleek vehicle. Marketers today are alert to these preferences;
- The social and cultural practices have an important influence on rural consumer behaviour. A marketer cannot ignore the influence of community on purchase and use behaviour as this can affect the product and the advertising message used. The presence of a community washing place would mean that washing soaps are not products used in private but used in front of others;
  Again, television viewing is still largely community viewing and hence rural audiences are not comfortable with sensuality or sexuality;
- Culture influences perceptions and behaviour. The preference for colour, size, shapes and taste are all influenced by culture. The perceptions of products vary because of these influences. An example of this is the perception of value according to size. Philips introduced large music systems instead of the compact ones it has for the urban markets;
- The influence of culture on communication is an important factor in promotion decisions. The importance and respect for elders influence the message source. The meaning that

symbols carry needs to be taken into account for promotion, e.g., marketers use names and symbols from the epic *Mahabharat* for promotion;

- The nature of occupation influences the marketers, strategy. Agricultural workers prefer to pay a smaller purchase price. This is because of the prevalence of the daily wage system. The popularity of small packs is a result of this;

- Rural institutions are different from those in urban areas. The social, political and economic institutions are significant for marketers. An important rural institution that influences marketing are the weekly village markets. Marketers use these markets to reach the rural consumers. Colgate–Palmolive uses the weekly village markets to promote its products.

Defining Rural Marketing and Rural Markets

A fairly large variety of transactions are considered as part of rural marketing. These can be categorized as follows:

- Marketing of agricultural inputs like fertilisers, pesticides, farm machinery etc;
- Marketing of products made in urban centres and sold to rural areas like soap, toothpaste, television sets, etc;
- Marketing of products made in rural areas sold to urban centres like khadi cloth, hand crafted products, etc; and
- Marketing of products made and sold in rural areas like milk and milk products, locally manufactured toothpowder, cloth, etc.

It is convenient to classify these transactions as exchange or flow between Rural and Urban locations. This will then result in four possible flows, shown in Figure 1.1 in two dimensions that result in four quadrants (Jha, 1999).

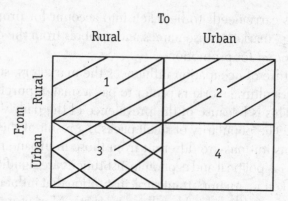

Figure 1.1 Types of Markets

Rural marketing excludes the Urban–Urban flow, i.e., quadrant 4, and could include quadrants 1, 2 or 3. The Rural–Rural flow is the marketing of products produced locally and is a relatively simple exchange management process. Managing the rural to urban flow has similarities with current marketing literature in that its focus is understanding the urban consumer, competition and channels serving that market. The focus of this book is therefore on box 3, Figure 1.1, the urban to rural flow, e.g., selling battery cells in rural areas.

Rural Market

The definition of rural marketing based on flows between rural and urban locations require defining the rural area. The definition that is best suited is the one used by the Census of India as it has advantages of relevance, simplicity and measurability (Jha, 1999):

Rural is defined as that which is not Urban. Urban is:

- All locations with a municipality/corporation, cantonment board or a notified town area;
- All other locations satisfying all of the following criteria:
  a) a minimum population of 5,000;

b) at least 75 percent of the male workforce engaged in non-agricultural activities; and

c) a population density of over 400 per sq. km.

Perspective Used

The decision maker's perspective is used throughout this book. A decision maker is required to understand the market, identify critical issues that need to be addressed and develop options to resolve these issues. These processes are examined for the rural marketing system. The elements of the rural marketing system include rural consumers, competitors in rural markets and the channel members serving the rural markets. The marketer is interested in understanding consumers and competition. Marketing options are relevant for the decision variables, which include product decisions, channel decisions, decisions on media, message and pricing decisions. To reflect these, the book is organised into:

- Environment of Rural Markets;
- Researching Rural Markets;
- Developing Suitable Value Proposition: Products and Price;
- Reaching Rural Markets;
- Competitive Strategy for Rural Markets.

The sequence reflects the need to look outwards at the environment of rural markets before examining options in each of the marketing decision areas. The strategic marketing decision integrates the decision variables to reflect the elements of the rural marketing system.

Decision Implications

The attitude towards rural market should be that of an investor. The growing market provides the opportunity. The approach is to be of 'market seeding'. The marketer has to invest to develop a separate marketing programme to meet the consumer needs.

The market provides opportunities and options for the rural marketer. The low penetration levels suggest opportunities. The marketer needs to have an information system that tracks the sales to different markets to identify potential. Improvements in infrastructure have created opportunities and the alert marketer is ready to develop concepts to meet the changing and growing consumer needs in the rural markets.

The marketer can use mass marketing or niche marketing to tap the potential. With knowledgeable and discriminating rural buyers, the suitable approach is to have product variants, differentiation and multiple brands.

References

Jha, Mithleshwar, 'Rural Marketing: Some Conceptual Issues', *Rural Scan*, Vol. 1, Issue 2, April 1999.

Law, Vivek, 'Rural India rings a bell for mobile majors', *The Economic Times*, December 21, 2000.

National Council of Applied Economic Research (NCAER), 'India Market Demographics Report, 1998', New Delhi.

Rai, Asha, 'Titan Chimes Rural Tunes with Sonata', *The Economic Times*, August 18, 2000.

TWO

The Rural Consumer

The focus of this chapter is on the buying behaviour of rural consumers. It covers lifestyles, behaviour variations and influences. Variations in lifestyle indicate opportunities for the marketer. Examining the lifestyle of the rural consumer helps to understand the consumption pattern and the influence of the environment on consumer behaviour. It has been found that products developed to meet the needs of the rural consumer are more widely accepted than products developed for urban markets. The influence of geography and occupation on consumer behaviour patterns is also examined. The rural consumer's place of purchase and product-use is diverse and also does not necessarily reflect the behaviour seen among urban consumers. Influences on rural consumer behaviour include the environment, cultural practices, perceptions and attitudes. The variations reflected in the design of the product and its message are the result of strategic marketing decision making.

Lifestyle of the Rural Consumer

The popular image of a rural consumer is of one who has limited educational background, is exposed to limited products and brands, choosing price over quality and is influenced by word-of-mouth communication. There is also the view that a rural consumer is no different from his urban counterpart. The changing consumption patterns reflect the evolving lifestyle of rural consumers. The increase in the purchase and use of products was noted while examining the growing importance of rural markets in the earlier chapter. The influences on the behaviour of the rural consumer is also changing. The lifestyle of rural consumers is influenced by:

- Increasing incomes and income distribution;
- Marketers efforts to reach out and educate potential consumers;
- The situation in which he or she utilizes the product.

This last point is usually an overriding factor. Understanding the product–use situation creates opportunities for marketers. This is because the rural environment does not have the infrastructure facilities available in urban areas which affects the consumption of both durable and non-durable products (see Box 2.1).

Box 2.1
Opportunities and Hurdles Created by Rural Needs

1. Many households in the rural area do not have electricity and this:
   (a) affects the ability of rural consumer to use electrical products; and
   (b) increases the demand for batteries.
2. The non-availability of piped running water affects both the durable and non-durable markets:
   (a) automatic washing machines have no demand in such situations;
   (b) washing powders cannot be used if clothes are washed in streams or ponds.
3. The availability of roads influences the purchase of motorised vehicles.
   In direct contrast:

- more than half the rural households own bicycles and mechanical wristwatches;
- about 42 percent of rural households have radios or transistors;
- of the 31 durables examined in a study by NCAER, six had penetration levels above 10 percent.

These situational factors are reflected in the data on consumption and use of products. They provide opportunities for marketers who are aware of the different demands in rural markets.

Distribution of Households by Income

It is short-sighted to view rural markets as an extension of urban markets. The issue facing the rural marketer is not of adequate consumers who can afford what the urban market consumes. The situation instead requires the marketer to identify and reach out to consumers with offers that meet variations in their ability to purchase.

In rural india, more than half the households are in the income category of less than Rs. 25,000 per annum but about 14 percent of the households have an annual income that exceeds Rs. 50,000 per annum (see Table 2.1 and Figure 2.1).

Table 2.1
Distribution of Households by Income

Annual Income (Rs.) at 1995–96 prices	Percentage
< 25,000 L	57.2
25,001–50,000 LM	29.0
50,001–77,000 M	8.6
77,001–1,06,000 UM	3.1
> 1,06,000–H	2.0
Total	100.00

Source: Natarajan (1998).

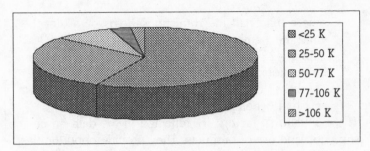

Figure 2.1 Distribution of Households by Annual Income

This distribution pattern is also true for three of the four regions of India. In Western India, there are approximately 45 percent of households with income levels below Rs. 25,000 per annum, and approximately 19 percent of households with income levels over Rs. 50,000 per annum (see Table 2.2).

Table 2.2
Distribution of Households by Income and by Region

(percentages)

Annual Income	North	South	East	West
< 25,000	57.26	61.35	61.94	44.56
25,001–50,000	27.20	27.11	27.38	36.79
50,001–77,000	9.41	7.51	6.99	11.27
77,001–1,06,000	3.18	2.72	2.33	4.71
> 1,06,000	2.94	1.30	1.36	2.67
Total	100.00	100.00	100.00	100.00

Source: Natarajan (1998).

The lack of electricity in many rural households acts as a barrier to consumer durables that require electricity. Re-defining the relevant population as 'rural households with electricity' instead of 'total rural households', would give a different picture of the ownership pattern of consumer durables. In this case, the average ownership of electrical goods jumps from 0.82 to 2.48 in the rural areas as compared to 3.39 in the urban areas. If

Table 2.3
Ownership of Durables

(per 1,000 households)

Product	Rural (1995–96)
Bicycle	529.0
Cassette recorder	173.2
Electric iron	82.7
Fan (ceiling)	190.5
Fan (table)	131.0
Geyser (instant)	0.3
Geyser (storage)	0.5
Mixer/grinder	31.2
Motorised 2 wheeler (moped)	17.7
Motorised 2 wheeler (motor cycle)	18.7
Motorised 2 wheeler (scooter)	21.1
Pressure cooker	130.3
Pressure pan	1.7
Radio/Transistor	418.9
Refrigerator	20.4
Sewing machine	65.4
TV (B&W)	154.8
TV (colour)	26.4
VCR/VCP	2.0
Washing machine	5.0
Wrist watch (mechanical)	759.7
Wrist watch (quartz)	257.5

Source: Natarajan (1998).

only households with electricity are considered for items like black and white televisions and cassette recorders, the rural penetration rate of these items would be higher than that of urban areas (see Table 2.3).

According to the study carried out by Natarajan (1998) (see Table 2.4), each household in the rural area owned on an average 2.2 non-electrical durables, with the lowest income bracket having 1.5 and highest income bracket owning approximately 5.4 non-electrical goods.

Table 2.4
Penetration of Non-electrical Consumer Durables by Income Group

Income Group	Percent of Households	Penetration per 1,000 Households
< 25,000 L	57.2	1,474
25,001–50,000 LM	29.0	2,649
50,001–77,000 M	8.6	3,463
77,001–1,06,000 UM	3.1	4,256
> 1,06,000 H	2.1	5,425
Total	100	2,155

Source: Natarajan (1998).

The average penetration level for electrical durables was slightly less than one per household (.9). As around 34 percent of rural households have electricity, the ownership of electrical products is about 2.6 per household (see Figure 2.2).

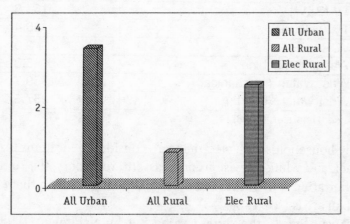

Figure 2.2 Ownership of Electrical Goods

Expenditure on Consumer Non-durables

Rural buyers consume certain non-durable products regularly, and this buying behaviour reflects their lifestyles. The rural household spends on an average, Rs. 3,203 per year for 22 consumer non-durables that include toiletries, cosmetics, packaged foods, washing products, etc. The average expenditure among rural households in the East was the lowest at Rs. 2,837 and in the West was the highest at Rs. 3,622 per annum for the 22 consumer non-durables. The rural household in the lowest income group spent Rs. 2,464 a year and the highest income group spent Rs. 8,021 a year (see Table 2.5 and Figure 2.3).

Table 2.5
Expenditure per Household for 22 Consumer Non-durables by Income Group

Income Group	Expenditure per Household (Rs.)
< 25,000 L	2,464
25,001–50,000 LM	3,474·
50,001–77,000 M	4,875
77,001–1,06,000 UM	6,422
> 1,06,000 H	8,021
Total	3,203

Source: Natarajan (1998).

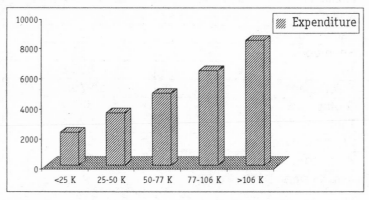

Figure 2.3 Expenditure per Household for Non-durables

Most rural households buy toilet soap, washing soap bars, edible oil and tea. Some non-durables like lipsticks, nail polish, health beverages and shampoo have very limited acceptance among rural consumers (see Table 2.6).

Table 2.6
Penetration Rates for 22 Consumer Non-durable Items among Rural Households

(purchasing households per 1,000 households)

Consumer Non-durable	No. of Households
Body talcum powder	368.5
Cigarettes	186.8
Face cream	148.2
Cooking medium (oil)	898.2
Cooking medium (vanaspati)	365.5
Electric bulbs	475.9
Electric tubes	109.6
Footwear (casual)	639.7
Footwear (leather)	502.9
Footwear (sports)	241.7
Hair oil/Cream	731.4
Health beverages	51.6
Lipstick	11.8
Nail polish	31.4
Packaged biscuits	231.1
Shampoo	81.0
Tea	835.8
Toilet soap	979.2
Toothpaste	329.7
Toothpowder	370.3
Washing cake	918.2
Washing powder	553.7

Source: Natarajan (1998).

The results from another study also support the above findings. According to this study:

1. Fast-moving consumer goods purchased by rural consumers include toilet soaps, washing soap bars, edible oil, tea and washing powders. These indicate that rural consumers buy basic products;

2. The acceptance of hair wash products like shampoos is less than products like soaps. This shows that personal hygiene is also considered important by a number of rural consumers.

3. The purchase of superior products is also indicated in this study. Toothpowders were considered to be the only sort of oral-care product rural consumers would buy, yet toothpaste penetration has actually overtaken toothpowder penetration (see Table 2.7).

Table 2.7
FMCG Penetration

FMCG Penetration Category	Total Penetration
Analgesics/cold/ethical tablets	27.9%
Batteries	21.3%
Bulbs	29.9%
Edible oils	84.7%
Hair wash products	39.4%
Iodized salt	61.5%
Safety razor blades	45.4%
Tea	79.1%
Toilet soaps	88.3%
Toothpowders	22.8%
Toothpaste	33.1%
Washing cakes/bars	87.5%
Washing powders/liquids	70.3%

Source: *Business World*, April 1999.

The Elusive Average for the Rural Consumer

A stereotype of the rural consumer or of rural consumer behaviour is absent and this creates problems as well as opportunities for the marketer. Variations in behaviour reflect geographical, demographical and behavioural influences on lifestyle which provides marketers with options to segment the market. The creative use of products suggests possibilities for market development. Behavioural bases for segmenting could be socio-cultural or consumer perceptions and attitudes.

Geographic Demographic Influences and Behaviour Variations

To understand rural buying behaviour, a marketer must first understand *a*) the factors that influence buying behaviour and *b*) the variations in behaviour. These help to generate information upon which a marketer can create bases to segment the rural market taking the following factors into consideration:

- Environment of the consumer;
- Geographical influences;
- Influence of occupation;
- Place of purchase;
- Creative use of products.

The behaviour variations that are unique to rural markets are influenced by the place of purchase and occupation and sometimes get reflected in the creative application or use of products.

Influence of the larger Environment on Rural Consumers

A villager's needs are different from those of an urban consumer. The environment is a critical influence in shaping the needs of rural consumers. Products made to urban specifications may be impractical in rural settings. An excellent example is that of electrical and electronic goods. Virtually all radios, cassette players and television sets are made to urban power supply specifications. In many villages, particularly in power-strapped states, voltages fluctuate wildly making electrical products susceptible to frequent breakdowns. Rural consumers may not mind paying more for products like the television or radio if they can withstand frequent voltage fluctuations.

Geographical Variations in Market Behaviour

The Rural Market is not a homogeneous one. Variations in economic development and in consumer willingness to accept innovations are evident in rural markets. Geographical variations in exposure to urban centres and variations in developement have resulted in tremendous heterogeneity even within a state, e.g., the difference between parts of western and eastern Uttar Pradesh is extreme.

Variations in consumer behaviour due to their geographical location is also reflected in the variations in their innovativeness. LML found that the south was more receptive to its scooters than the north. In the words of their Marketing Manager, Rakesh Jayal,'people in the south are more willing to accept a high-tech product than in the north. They are more brand conscious, more educated' (Das Gupta and Menon, 1990). A variation in the behaviour of buyers of watches between rural areas of the north and of the south is also evident (see Box 2.2).

Box 2.2
Behaviour Variations of Watch Buyers

The demand for watches is high in rural areas and it increases during the marriage season. This is true throughout the country. The variation is however in the type of watch and brand that is preferred by the consumers. In the villages of the north, 'winding' watches are preferred which

---

are bought from large feeder villages nearby. The awareness of quartz brands of watches is limited. The awareness
of a brand is usually from newspapers in addition to word
of mouth.

In the south, the preference is for a quartz watch and is
purchased from a showroom in the town. In some villages,
television has created a high degree of product awareness.
As the purchase of quartz watches is expensive, the villager
prefers to buy it from the town and is also willing to take it
back to the showroom in town in the event there is a
problem with the watch.

Occupation and Consumption Pattern

The perception that the rural consumer is either a farmer or
an agricultural labourer restricts marketing effectiveness. In
fact there are other groups of consumers with different needs
and behaviour and having significant purchase volumes.

IRS, '98 has chosen the occupation of the chief wage earn-
er as a basis to define the rural consumer. Occupation profiles of owners of three popular consumer durables indicate
that the non-agricultural occupation groups of shopkeepers
or traders and those employed in service (government administration jobs, banks, teachers, etc.) are the high consumption
segment. Television owners in the service class is 43 percent,
which means one in two persons owns a television set. In the
case of the other non-agricultural group, the shopkeepers and
traders, one in three own a television.

Land-owning farmers comprise a mere one-third of
rural households (their estimated number being 43.2 million
households) and own one-third of these durables. Shopkeepers
and the service occupation on the other hand, together account
for just 21 percent of the rural households (their estimated
number is 26.8 million households) but between them own a
disproportionately higher number (between 45 and 60 percent
of televisions, two-wheelers and refrigerators. To put this group

Table 2.8
Occupation and Consumption Patterns

Occupation Category	Percentage in Rural Households	Percentage Contribution to Television Ownership	Percentage Contribution to Rural Two-wheeler Ownership	Percentage Contribution to Refrigerators
Owner farmer	34	33	33	31
Shop keeper/trader	8	14	16	20
Service (total)	13	31	39	40
Inside village	5	11	15	15
Outside village	8	20	24	25
Agricultural worker	20	6	3	2
Unskilled non-agricultural labour	17	9	4	5
Artisan	6	6	4	2
Rest (leased farmers, livestock, poultry, fishery, milkman)	2	2	1	1

Source: Bijapurkar and Murthy, 1999

in perspective, they are 27 million households in number, which is more than half of all urban households (see Table 2.8) (Bijapurkar and Murthy, 1999).

Place of Purchase Variations: Not all rural consumers buy from the same location. It is also true that the same consumer could buy from different locations depending on the product and the need. A study on *haats* indicates that, despite the same product being available in the village shop, 58 percent of the rural consumers visiting the *haats* preferred to buy these from the *haat* because of better prices, quality and variety (Kashyap, 1998).

Rural consumers do not rely on the local outlets and *haats* alone, as some of the purchases are made in the urban areas (see Figure 2.4). This is because:

- There are a few product categories where rural distribution is still comparatively low and therefore the consumer buys from towns; and
- In certain cases, the consumer seeks variety. In the case of toilet soaps and washing powders, the range in villages may be perceived as limited by the consumers.

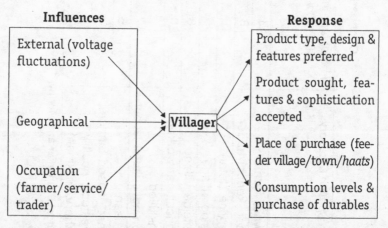

Figure 2.4 Influences on Behaviour and its Implications

Table 2.9
Percentage of Products bought from Nearby Towns

Category	Percentage Share from Urban Purchase
Shaving preparations	36.6
Bulbs and balms	32.0
Toilet soaps	24.0
Washing powders/liquids	23.4
Iodized salt	14.4

Source: *Business World*, April 1999.

Social and Behavioural Influences

The rural consumer is influenced by the environment and also by his or her wants and perceptions. Understanding the social and attitudinal influences on rural consumer behaviour is important to the marketer, as these serves as a guide to decisions on product offering, pricing, distribution, media and message; in effect forming the 'rural marketing strategy' (see Figure 2.5).

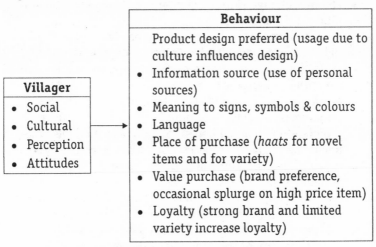

Villager
- Social
- Cultural
- Perception
- Attitudes

Behaviour
Product design preferred (usage due to culture influences design)
- Information source (use of personal sources)
- Meaning to signs, symbols & colours
- Language
- Place of purchase (*haats* for novel items and for variety)
- Value purchase (brand preference, occasional splurge on high price item)
- Loyalty (strong brand and limited variety increase loyalty)

Figure 2.5 Social and Behavioural Influences

Cutural Social Practices and Consumer Behaviour

The cultural and social practices have a major influence on the behaviour of the rural consumer. The widely dispersed villages and limited communication helped preserve traditions in rural markets. Increasing access to urban areas and information dissemination possibly reduces the influence of traditions (see Box 2.4).

Box 2.4
Is Tradition Giving Way to Modernity?

In the traditional scenario, decision making on a purchase was limited to the male heads of households. An increase in rural literacy coupled with greater access to information has resulted in the involvement of the other members of the family in purchase decision making. This presents a wider target audience for marketing and wider media options for advertisers.

An increased exposure of rural consumers to urban lifestyles has led to a gradual change in norms and roles prevalent in the social fabric of viallges.

- A primary symptom of the change is the shift from collective thought to individual acction.
- Another change is in the similarities in perceptions, attitudes and benefits.

  Arun Adhikari of HLL says 'Media has taught rural India to learn to decode the advertising structure and has build aspirations.... In a commercial's content, there are more similarities emerging than dissimilarities for broad based products'. An example: Lux runs the same advertising film across markets. As a brand and in its advertising, it promotes a functional benefit of 'pure and mild'. Its emotional cue of glamour and escape rubs well with consumers who are socially trapped, i.e., both city and rural audiences' (Arathoon, M. 1999).
- A third change is in the behaviour of the rural consumer. The saving and investment patterns of the rural rich is shifting from gold and land to tractors, harvesters, video cassette recorders and Maruti cars (Kashyap, 1998).

Till such time that cultural influences persist, the marketer has to:

- Develop products that suit the cultural practices of the rural consumer;
- Identify a suitable target audience and design media and message that reflect social behaviour;
- Design the distribution to reach the places or outlets from where the consumer has been traditionally making his purchase.

The influence of culture reveals itself in consumer preferences for product features, product size, shape and colour. For instance, the preference for large audio equipment is a reflection of this influence. The information source is also influenced by social practices. Since villages have a common washing area, purchases like toilet soap and toothpaste, which are usually private in an urban household, are known to all. It provides immense status to brush your teeth with a toothpaste or use a detergent to wash clothes (Joshi, 1991).

An important social and cultural phenomenon is the *mela*. *Melas* are a prominent feature of Indian rural life, held periodically or annually to commemorate important events or to honour a diety. Farmers flush with funds after a harvest frequent *melas* with their families. Women, who are ordinarily restricted from moving out of the village, have universal social sanction to visit the *mela*.

A marketer's response to the influence of cultural and social practices is in the areas of product and of promotion. Marketers design products to reflect social and cultural influences. The message to promote products makes use of the signs and symbols the villager is familiar with (see Box 2.5).

Box 2.5
How Cultural and Social Practices Influence Marketing Decisions on Products and Promotions

- One company which succeeded in selling the same product in different markets simply by changing the packaging, is the West Bengal based KMP Oils. In Muslim-dominated Uttar Pradesh, the company's hair oil is sold in green packs. In Orissa, the same packs come in purple as this colour is considered auspicious.
- Murphy discovered that the name 'Murphy Manna' was well accepted by rural consumers.
- Texla cashed in on the popularity of the 'Mahabharat' serial by naming its sets 'Arjun and Yuvraj'.
- Dabur distributes religious texts like the 'Hanuman Chalisa' and 'Ramcharitmanas' or calendars with religious themes along with its ayurvedic products (Das Gupta and Menon, 1990).

Perception and its Influence on Product Design and Message

The marketer who seeks to modify the behaviour of the rural consumer needs to first influence perception and attitude. It is here that the marketer has to be careful in designing products and developing a message for the rural market. The decision variables of product and message are critical to marketing effectiveness in rural markets as the colour, shape and actions hold meaning for rural consumers that are different from those held by urban consumers.

A consumer's interpretation of product and promotion contribute to creating the position for the product. The interpretations of the rural consumer differ from those of the urban consumers. Colours are interpreted differently, so are sizes and shapes. The lower literacy levels in the rural market increase the importance of perceptual influences. In interior markets brand identification is through visual patterns—a red soap cake signifies Lifebuoy soap. The strong influence of perceptions on rural consumers provide a good reason for the marketer to develop a separate marketing strategy for the rural market (see Box 2.6).

Box 2.6
Perceptions Suggest Rural Market Strategies different from those for Urban Markets

Philips sells their products on account of size rather than sound to the rural market. Consumers are willing to pay a higher price for larger machines, on the assumption that big must be better. The company now makes its rural models one and a half times larger and louder than the ones for urban markets (Mukherjee, 1993).

Attitude to Quality and Price

Conventional wisdom on rural marketing believes that the villager craves, but can't afford the products his city cousin consumes. As a result, companies usually try to reduce the prices of their products either by creating smaller pack sizes, or by compromising on quality. This works sometimes, and with some products.

Small pack sizes get acceptance in markets which can pay only a small price because of the nature of income receipts. A landless labourer may get a small amount of money everyday, so he buys his provisions daily and does not have a big amount to spend. He will therefore buy something that has a small unit price. The introduction of the sachet pack for instance, led to a boom in shampoo sales during the eighties. Hindustan Lever found that retailers in villages were cutting its large 100 gm. soap into smaller pieces and selling these, so it introduced a small 75 gm. soap (Joshi, 1991).

It is not true that only cheap brands sell in rural markets. Usha found that the sale of its economy models were falling sharply in rural areas. Farmers prefer Usha's premier Century brand, though it is priced 20 percent higher (Das Gupta and Menon, 1990).

Brand Preference and Loyalty

A marketer does not perceive an opportunity in the rural market when he or she is aware that the rural consumer buys un-branded items. It is useful to have a good understanding of the purchase behaviour of the consumer in order to guide decisions in the rural markets. In as many as 18 product categories, consumption of branded items account for 80 percent of sales (see Table 2.10). These are not always national brands, regional or locally manufactured brands also have good sales. This indicates the potential for national brands if they can find a way to package their offering to compete effectively with regional brands.

The attitude of the rural consumers favours quality products and brands but brand pricing has to take into account both the income-level and income-flow of the consumers. The rural consumers, as seen earlier, are not homogenous. There are consumers who can afford high priced brands. A group of rural consumers can not only afford, but are also willing to buy, high priced brands (see Table 2.11).

Table 2.10
Preference for Brands

Percent Branded	< 20 %	21–40 %	41–60 %	61–80 %	81–100 %
Necessity	Non-refined oil		Iodized salt Tea Washing cakes	Biscuits	Toilet soaps Washing powder
Popular		Coconut oil		Blues	Analgesics Safety razor blades Toothpastes Shampoos
Premium				Vanaspati Bulbs Hair oils	Batteries Rubs & Balms Skin creams Toothpowders
Super-premium		Refined oil	Home insecticides		Toothbrushes Antiseptic creams Antiseptic liquids *Chyavanprash* Digestives Mosquito repellants Shaving preparations Tubelights

Source: *Business World*, April 7–12, 1999.

Table 2.11
Penetration of High Priced Brands of
Washing Powders and Toilet Soaps

Washing Powders	Penetration (% of households)
Surf	6.7
Wheel	15.0
Nirma	45.7

Toilet Soaps	Penetration (% of households)
Lifebuoy	31.9%
Breeze	10.3%
Lux	2.4%
Pears	1.2%

Source: *Business World*, April 7–12, 1999.

Brand loyalty

Multi-brand strategies and entry for new brands in rural markets are possible, though it is perceived to be a highly brand loyal market. The rural consumer is willing to consider alternatives. The loyalty of rural consumers to a brand varies according to product categories. Loyalty is low in toilet soaps, toothpaste, batteries and washing cakes but high in home insecticides, *chyavanprash*, shaving preparations and skin creams. Brand loyalty is possibly lower in product categories where there is more choice and not much brand building (see Table 2.12).

Table 2.12
Loyalty Levels

Category	% Loyalty*	Category	% Loyalty
Analgesics/cold/ ethical tablets	21.8	Rubs & Balms	47.2
Batteries	17.7	Safety razor blades	26.5
Biscuits	22.8	Shaving preparations	67.3
Bulbs	32.8	Skin creams	62.5

Table 2.12 Contd.

Table 2.12 Contd.

Chyavanprash	77.3	Tea	25.3
Coconut oil	52.1	Toilet soaps	3.1
Hair wash preparations	28.9	Toothpowders	47.3
Home insecticides	85.8	Toothpastes	12.6
Iodized salt	24.2	Washing cakes/bars	18.0
		Washing powders/ Liquids	25.9

* Loyalty is defined as buying only a single brand every time the category is purchased in the last six months
Source: *Business World*, April 7–12, 1999.

Rural consumers also exhibit the use of multiple brands within a household. It is highest among toilet soaps and washing cakes (see Table 2.13).

Table 2.13
Multiple Brand usage in Rural Households

Category	% Multiple User Households*	Category	% Multiple User Households*
Analgesics/ cold/ethical tablets	27.6	Safety razor blades	16.1
Batteries	8.2	Tea	26.0
Biscuits	28.8	Toilet soaps	42.9
Bulbs	12.0	Toothpowders	6.3
Digestives	11.6	Toothpastes	8.6
Edible oils	15.4	Washing cakes/ bars	30.7
Hair wash preparations	22.8	Washing powders/ liquids	21.9
Rubs & Balms	10.1		

* Multiple users are those who have bought more than one brand in a category in the last month.
Source: *Business World*, April 7–12, 1999.

The Gap in Understanding

It is well established that consumers in rural areas are different from consumers in urban areas. The rural market itself is diverse with vastly different behaviour across different geographical locations or across buyer groups. The rural consumers also have their share of rich and poor. Their purchases reflect their incomes, physical environment, their cultural and social practices, perceptions and attitudes. The place of purchase of a product and product-usage vary according to consumers, products, and situations and add to the complexity in the behaviour of the rural consumer. The sophistication in approach to the rural markets is clearly a necessity and starts with the recognition of the non-existence of the average rural consumer. This calls upon the marketer to invest time and effort to understand the rural consumer. This suggests that research on specific markets of interest is required for meaningful marketing decisions. The regular monitoring of consumer purchase and use behaviour is critical to avoid surprises.

Creative Use of Products

The marketer will find it fruitful to keep track of the different ways in which the product is used by the rural consumer. This is because the product use could differ and may not be as envisaged by the marketer. Even for the experienced marketer surprises never cease. Market development is achieved by being alert to the new and creative uses for the product (see Box 2.7).

The gap in understanding of the consumer behaviour and the creative use that consumers exhibit suggest researching consumer behaviour and monitoring consumer use. These are the subject matter in Chapter 3.

Box 2.7
Consumer Surprises Marketer with
Innovative Use of Products

Pratap Roy of Godrej travelled to Islampur, a remote village in Maharashtra, by his company's van. After the usual hoopla—music, the announcement of free gifts etc., the van made its way to the few shops in the village. There was a surprise in store for him: every shopkeeper wanted to lay his hands on all the bottles of hair dye available. Roy discovered that the farmers who bought from the shops did not want the dye for themselves. They were using it to colour their cattle to make them look younger and healthier (Das Gupta and Menon, 1990)!

Decision Implications

The rural market differs by geography, occupation and social and cultural factors. This in turn influences product design, promotion, pricing and use of channels. There is a need to therefore develop positioning and product variants according to the geography and social grouping. Occupation is useful to prioritise the sequence for market entry, with the initial focus on a service group. The product offering in rural markets needs to reflect the product–use situation, e.g., electrical products should withstand frequent voltage fluctuations.

Thus, the marketing programme should be guided by consumer behaviour. Understanding and monitoring use behaviour of consumers helps to discover new uses for products. This is useful for market development. The product design, packaging and promotional efforts need to take into account the signs and symbols the villager is familiar with. The colour, size and shape has to contribute to the desired positioning. The use of a higher price as a message for quality is useful for high value items, while for non-durables the important aspect is the pack size. Channel decisions depends on the product category. Rural consumers prefer to buy different products from different locations. Traditional outlets like *haats* are important for some of the higher priced non-durables. Consumers seek variety for such products and therefore the marketer will find it effective to deliver the product to the *haats*. The changing behaviour of a segment of rural markets suggest an initial entry strategy of mimicking the urban marketing programme, but this has limits to growth.

References

Arathoon, Marion, 'It's the same world after all', *Brand Equity, The Economic Times*, October 6–12, 1999.

Bijapurkar, R. and Murthy, Ravi, 'Rural Markets for Consumer Durables', *The Economic Times*, August 16, 1999.

Business World, 'The Undiscovered Country', April 7–12, 1999.

Das Gupta, Surajeet and Menon, Ramesh, 'The Call of Consumerism' *India Today*, July 15, 1990.

Ghosh, Aparisim, 'The New Rules of Rural Marketing', *Business World*, April 6–19 1994.

Joshi, Anjali, 'The New El Dorado', *The Sunday Observer*, April 28–May 4, 1991.

Kashyap, Pradeep, 'Selling to the sons of the soil', *Strategic Marketing*, Volume 1, Issue 4, Aug–Oct 1998.

Mukherjee, Biman, 'The Fairground as Battlefield', *Business Today*, December 7–21 1993.

Natarajan, I, 'India Market Demographics Report, 1998', New Delhi: National Council of Applied Economic Research, 1998.

THREE

Researching Rural Markets

This chapter examines research design options relevant for understanding rural markets. A reference frame appropriate to research rural markets is by comparisons with urban markets. The process reflects the philosophy of understanding the unknown based on a comparison with the known. The research approach that makes use of the rural consumer's frame of reference is considered appropriate for rural markets. These methods avoid using the urban frame of reference to understand the rural mind. The 'Participatory Rural Appraisal' is one such method where the dimensions for a given research objective are developed by the consumers as are the measures for understanding behaviour. The possible biases while sampling for rural markets are also identified.

Sensitizing Research to Rural Markets

The research process is critical to rural marketing. There are two reasons for this:

1. The marketer has a limited understanding of the rural consumer; and
2. The marketer who is urban oriented may find it useful to unlearn consumer response to decision variables in the

urban market. This requires the use of research methodology that is sensitive to social processes in rural markets.

The research process used in urban markets may not always be appropriate in rural markets. Selecting the research process therefore requires care in application. Alternative methods to research rural markets, including options on design, measures and sampling are examined below.

Research Design

Appropriate research design is examined at two levels:

1. A reference frame for understanding the rural consumers; and
2. A suitable research approach: methods of experiments, survey and case studies are evaluated for their suitability to rural markets

Reference Frame

When researching rural markets, urban markets are generally used as the reference point. In this way a known phenomenon, the urban market, is used as the standard to examine and measure different aspects of the relatively unknown phenomenon, the rural market. This approach helps understand perceptions, attitudes and preferences among the rural consumers (Velayudhan, 1995). The use of this approach is common and one study that examined the behaviour of consumers of soap made use of this. A study of the behaviour of rural consumers of soap was greatly aided by examining the urban consumers of soap on the same variables. Points of similarity and of variations provide directions for decision making (Velayudhan, 1998).

Research Approach

The research approach used is critical in rural markets. The options generally considered are the experimental, survey or case study approach.

• The experimental approach is relevant for understanding causation. This restricts its application in rural markets.
• The case study and survey approach therefore, find greater application here.
  – case studies of individuals to understand their purchase behaviour cost higher in terms of time and money; and
  – given the absence of information and the difficulty to get rural respondents to articulate their perception, attitudes and behaviour, an indepth form of survey is the preferred option.

Experimental Approach

An experimental approach is appropriate in situations where the information required is of a specific nature. This method was used to understand the influence of brand names on perceptions and attitudes (see Box 3.1).

Box 3.1
Impact of Brand Name Changes

A leading watch company wanted to enter the rural market with one of its cheaper watches. It wanted to continue to use the sub-brand name, but drop its umbrella brand name. The company was not sure of its impact on the sales of the product line. It then conducted an experiment by selecting two matched groups of respondents. They were exposed to a number of advertisements, out of which one was of the watch. One group was exposed to an advertisement without the umbrella brand name and the other with the umbrella brand name. The scores on recall, perception of quality and preference were not significantly different between the two groups of respondents.

Indepth Survey

An indepth survey also requires the use of measures to capture consumer perceptions, attitudes and preferences. It also however, allows flexibility in understanding rural markets. The advantage of this is that the involvement of respondents is higher and incorrect understanding of behaviour due to errors created by language, signs and symbols are also minimized.

Diffusion of Innovations

The methods used here are useful to marketers in product development and design. These include:

- The study of existing products; and
- The use of extension centres for:
  - indepth interviews; and
  - feedback on prototype.

Study of Existing Products: This approach requires the systematic examination of the product currently used by the consumer to meet his/her need. The design features provide useful insights on certain usage patterns, skills and habits of the users. These provide valuable inputs on design and features to be incorporated. It also provides information on product weaknesses that need to be addressed.

Use of Extension Centres: The use of extension centres provides an opportunity to gather information from villagers easily. The consumers familiarity with the interviewer or institution reduces the rural consumer's inhibition to provide information. The extension centers are useful in carrying out indepth surveys.

It is also useful to build prototypes for trial use by the respondents in an actual setting. This feedback is very useful for product design. The relevance of the product can then be examined for the consumer by testing the product at these extension centres.

This approach to designing products for the rural market is observed in diffusion studies. Its application is seen for developing a fuel efficient wood stove (see Box 3.2).

Box 3.2
ASTRA *Ole*

ASTRA or the Application of Science and Technology in Rural Areas is a cell in the Indian Institute of Science, Bangalore. *Ole* is the word for stove in Kannada, the language spoken in Karnataka.

Most rural households use wood for cooking fuel requirements. The deforestation adversely affected the availability of wood as fuel and this became a problem for rural households. One option to meet this problem was to develop a fuel efficient wood stove.

A study of the traditional woodstove suggested the development and design problem to be examined. The need to improve the efficiency of the traditional stove from approximately 9 percent was recognized. A discussion with potential users at the extension centre in Ungra village (Kunigal Taluk, Tumkar district, Karnataka state) ended with suggestions for a number of features: They suggested that their ideal stove should:

1. Have a shape and overall size that was similar to traditional stoves;
2. Preferably be made from materials available locally;
3. Allow the use of agricultural residues like coconut or arecanut husks, twigs, bagasse, etc., apart from the main fuel, viz. firewood in the form of twigs, branches and cut wood;
4. Disperse smoke away from the cooking zone and the interior of the house;
5. Be easy to light and extinguish, need little attention and not require many adjustments to yield good results;
6. Be cheap and easy to construct; and
7. Not demand significant changes in the food habits and traditional cooking practices of the villagers.

The redesigned woodstove realized about 50 percent thermal efficiency. This resulted from three design features:

1. A grate for the entry of primary air to the combustion zone;
2. Increased combustion temperatures by controlling and optimising excess air; and
3. Improved heat transfer efficiency by proper dimensional and structural design of the flue passages with respect to the pans.

The final design included a grate to a shielded combustion chamber, primary and secondary air vents to ensure complete combustion, and a chimney to provide a draught and remove exhaust gases from the interior of the house. The cooking habits of most users was taken into account and this influenced the number of pans that the stove could hold. As the redesigned stove had only a single combustion chamber for all three pans, this stove required a modification of cooking practices.

The study of the existing wood stove also suggested the size of the pan to be used in designing the stove. Building the stove locally was suggested to make the best use of local material. To retain critical design aspects for thermal efficiency some of the items were manufactured and supplied. The programme resulted in a fuelwood stove having the following features:

1. Suitability for use with a variety of bio-mass fuels;
2. Higher fuel efficiency and therefore lower fuel consumption;
3. Lower cooking times; and
4. A smokeless operation.

Source: Krishnaswamy, K.N et al

Development Studies

Examining literature on development studies to understand behaviour among the rural population provides research methodology options for rural markets. A relevant approach used in such a context is a method called the Participatory Rural Appraisal (PRA). The PRA is applied to study the behaviour of cattle farmers in their purchase of inputs for cattle rearing and in their sale of milk produce (see Box 3.3). The case study is followed by a description of the PRA method.

Box 3.3
Cattle Owner Behaviour: Purchase of Inputs and Sale of Milk

To understand the behaviour of cattle owners in the purchase and use of feed and other inputs (products and services), a study was carried out. The study used both an intensive interactive approach and also structured interviews. The interactive approach (PRA.) involved a number of steps:

1. The first was to decide on the venue where the interaction was to take place. To select a suitable venue, the help of an important person in the 'Village Milk Producer's Society' was taken.
2. Next was an informal stroll around the village to observe the presence and type of cattle, the surroundings (type of shed and hygiene), the feed used and the kind of homes that owned the cattle. Informal discussions with some of the villagers threw more light on feeding and cattle rearing practices, the type of cattle in the village and viability of rearing cattle.
3. The third step involved establishing rapport and understanding the village and its resources. After an initial discussion with farmers, they were encouraged to draw a map of the village and its resources on a flip chart. This helped identify the households with cattle, the presence of grasslands, the veterinary centre, Milk Producer's Society and other institutions in the village.
4. The fourth step involved collection of additional data required for the study. The data collection methods used were such that the villagers developed the dimensions relevant to their context using methods and measures that they understood.

To understand the activities according to the time of the year, the villagers developed their own season or time-scale.

The villagers were asked to divide the year in their own terms—season-wise, month-wise or any other way—and record seasonally varying information about livestock, especially cattle, such as:

- Timing of herd movements
- Time spent by men and women
- Absence/presence of seasonal labour force
- Forage (food for cattle) use and availability
- Seasonality of animal disease
- Purchase/sale of livestock inputs
- Livestock births—seasonality and milk availability
- Livestock related income and expenditure
- Prices of livestock, their products

These were indicated by them through pictures or symbols on a flip chart.

The perceptions on different dimensions developed by them were captured using a matrix structure. The villagers were then asked to indicate different aspects like availability and preferences for various inputs like forage, health and artificial insemination services, medicines etc. The scores were in the form of 'dots', with the highest score having five dots and the least one dot. Some of the items were :

1. **Inputs**   **Dry fodder**   **Grass**   **Cattle feed**
   - availability
     throughout year
   - availability
     during season
   - price during season
   - yield of cattle

2. For cattle feed some of the aspects examined included:
   Brands   **A**   **B**   **C**
   - preference of cattle
   - yield
   - availability
   - price

PRA Approach: This method is extensively used in development studies. It is a method in which the involvement of the respondents or rural consumers is very high. The method involves a number of steps:

1. To identify a location which facilitates discussion and increases the likelihood of getting respondents;
2. Walking through the village (called a 'transect' walk), helps to familiarize the researcher with the surroundings. It provides an opportunity for observation on some of the issues and elicits views in an informal manner;
3. Village mapping (location and resources) on a flip chart, on the ground, black board or even the use of *rangoli* powder helps to start the discussions and gives a better understanding of the village and its key resources;
4. Using a number of tools to capture additional data. These include:

   - **Time line** requires getting the villagers to prepare a chronology of major events and activities. Using their understanding of the past captures events significant to them;
   - **Seasonality diagram** is used to break up information by seasons and therefore obtain greater clarity from the information available;
   - **Matrix Ranking** is used to capture perceptions, attitudes and preferences. The relative measures are obtained through objects like stones or the use of symbols. The larger the number of objects or symbols, the greater is the intensity of the phenomena;
   - **Venn diagrams** (also called *chapatis*) are used to identify various entities (individuals and organisations) relevant to the issue and to indicate their relative importance based on the size of the circles.

Data collection and interaction with villagers requires establishing rapport. It is generally recommended that the visit should be for at least two days. The first day is to get to know the villagers and establish a rapport. If the marketer can stay in the village, the rapport is easily established. The second day will be then more productive in gathering information.

The Need for PRA: The advantage of this method is derived from the philosophy that guides it. Understanding of the respondents is not to be led by the researcher's frame of reference but of that of the respondents, i.e., not address them on the basis of 'our' perception and 'their' needs but to try and understand *their* perception of *their* needs.

The focus of PRA is to involve the respondents in not only sharing information or data but also in creating the method to record the data. The consumer behaviour or needs are therefore captured using the respondent's frame of reference. This is indicated in the study performed for a milk processing and marketing unit (MPMU).

MPMU is a unit for procuring, processing and marketing milk and milk products under the cooperative sector in one of the southern states in India. It provides inputs to cattle owners like feeds, veterinary support and medicines, procures milk and markets milk and milk products. It faced price competition from smaller dairies. The lower prices to consumers offered by the small dairies could be sustained because of their low overheads. The small dairies also provided a higher price to the suppliers. As a result of the competition on price, MPMU was losing its market share. MPMU's response was to increase the procurement price to maintain supplies and in order to retain the already low margins it had to increase its consumer price. The ability of smaller dairies to compete increased with higher margins. It was assumed that price was the main consideration for the supplier. The information obtained using a questionnaire survey, supported the contention that the selling price of milk was critical to the cattle owner. PRA however indicated that the cattle owner was more concerned with the returns than just the selling price of milk. The cattle owner was more concerned with inputs as he faced difficulties in procuring them. He was keen on getting the right feed at reasonable prices, veterinary help and medicines when needed and at his place than just the price received for the milk. MPMU provided these services, which other smaller dairies could not. As the only variable that was being emphasized was price, the farmer sought a higher price for the milk he supplied to MPMU. What was required was improving the quality and effectiveness of service to the farmers, as originally envisaged. All that was required was to go back to its original ideals, which provided the basis for a viable system.

Sampling

In the case of sampling, generally stratified or quota sampling is used. A random method is used to identify villages that are representative. After the villages are selected a marketer has two options:

1. To survey the entire village;
2. Select respondents randomly after listing all the villagers.

For surveys that use structured interviews, dimensions need to be obtained on different aspects. This requires in-depth interviews with villagers, which give a better understanding of the situation. The results of the survey using structured interviews should not normally conflict with the inference from indepth interviews.

Operational Aspects of Data Collection

Care must be exercised in operational aspects that may result in:

1. Distortion of sample characteristics;
2. Distortion in the data recorded;
   - while collecting data, it is best to focus on collecting the information and to avoid being presumptious.

3. In the case of sampling again, it is better to avoid bias like:
   - road side bias: as an interior village is difficult to access, visit a road side village;
   - big farmer bias: a big farmer is responsive and he influences others to respond;
   - literacy bias: the farmer is educated and therefore understands concepts better and it is therefore easier to get information from him;
   - gender bias: Males are easier to access therefore it is easier to get information from them;
   - seasonal bias: as it is hot in summer, surveys are carried out in cooler months.

Decision Implications

A researcher of rural markets will find it useful to have a research design that compares urban and rural markets, as this will help draw a meaningful inference between the two. The research design should also reflect rural consumer behaviour. The research methods used in development studies are relevant for researching rural markets. The Participatory Rural Appraisal (PRA) is a suitable method. In this method dimensions and measures are identified by the respondent instead of being imposed by the researcher.

Generally, indepth interviews are preferred over structured interviews or questionnaires. Indepth interviews increase the validity of the data obtained as they allow the respondent flexibility to express an opinion within the frame of reference. Marketers can use experimental methods in rural markets for decisions on specific aspects like responses to brand names, packaging, specific attributes and pricing. The validity is increased by using visual cues and obtaining behaviour as the response. Research for decisions on product features require that products that are in use be studied. The use habits and practices are reflected in the design of products currently used by consumers.

In the sampling method, one approach is to select a respresentative village. The sample within the selected villages can be such as to reflect the profile of the village population. A marketer can get support, better response rate and quality of response if extension centres of organisations such as NGOs are used. This is particularly useful for product testing.

References

Krishnaswamy, K.N., Balaji, G. and Reddy, A.K.N., 'Case study of ASTRA *Ole* wood stove', Workshop on Utilization of Rural Technology, International Development Research Centre, New Delhi, October 5–6, 1998.

Velayudhan, Sanal Kumar, 'Urban Reference and Divided Rural Market: Search for a framework', *Indian Journal of Marketing*, Vol. 24, No. 4, 1995.

Velayudhan, Sanal Kumar, 'Buyer Behaviour in Rural Markets: A Study of Soap Market', *Productivity*, Vol. 39, No. 2, July–September, 1998.

FOUR

Value Offering

This chapter examines the decision variables of a product and its price. These two variables determine the net value for the rural consumer. Product market decisions are required to effectively use the resources in rural markets. This is important given the different products targeted at different segments in the rural market. The use of critical strengths of the organization to effectively serve the target market segments is examined. The use of product features as evidence in positioning the offer is also discussed in this chapter.

The consumer's perception of value in the context of rural markets suggests developing product features, packaging and pricing that truly reflect their needs. This is evident in the success of even a minor innovation like the introduction of sachets for shampoos.

Product and Price as Strategic Variables

A marketing strategy for rural markets focuses on products tailored to the needs of these consumers. The other option is to offer a low-priced product targeted at price sensitive rural consumers. The choice of strategy depends on the organisations' ability to meet the consumer needs effectively. This requires delivering value to the consumers by developing suitable products at a price they are willing to pay and at a place where they can conveniently purchase (see Figure 4.1). The critical components of *product* and *price* that influence value are discussed here.

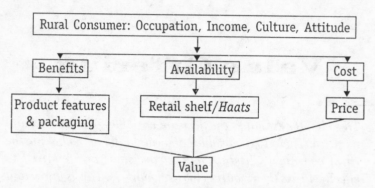

Figure 4.1 Product and Price as Critical Factors

Product strategy decisions include product–market selection and positioning. Decisions on the product range and its features are required to support the selected product–market and the positioning. These decision areas are examined here.

Product–Market Selection

Marketers may offer a number of products to the rural market. For a specific product, a variation in the needs of the rural market provides segmentation opportunities. The marketer must therefore prioritise the products and segments within the rural market to target marketing efforts. This allocation of effort is based upon the relative ability to utilize opportunities in different product–markets.

Differing consumer needs and perceptions provide opportunities to marketers. Modern means of communication have less influence on cultural and social practices in rural areas than in urban areas. Variations between rural markets in different states are therefore much more pronounced. The development and launch of a smokeless *chulha* or wood-burning stove in Karnataka is an example. It was discovered that even the number, size and shape of pan holders in the stove varied between districts.

The ability to utilize the opportunities in rural markets depend among others, on:

- Cost-effectiveness; and
- The reach of distribution of products in the rural markets.

Reach is a critical factor in effectively serving the different product–markets in rural areas. Nirma was the first to tap the opportunity in the rural market for detergent powder through its catchy promotion. However, when Wheel, another detergent powder, was introduced in the same market, it created a dent in Nirma's market indicating the potency of an effective strategy based on channel resources.

Product–market selection decisions in rural markets require a careful assessment of relative capabilities on distribution and the cost of the offering. These capabilities influence the ability to tap market opportunities better than the competition in rural markets. Matching these capabilities with market needs helps decide the allocation of efforts among the product–markets.

Product Range

Rural markets are not homogeneous. This clearly suggests the need for creating and offering product variants to meet the different needs within the rural markets. The successful attempt at packaging variations of KMP Oils to suit the colour preferences of different buyer groups is one such example.

A study of the rural markets for toilet soap in one of the states in South India suggests that a wide product range is required to tap differing consumer needs. The study discovered that certain families used a single brand of toilet soap while many other families used multiple brands. In some families that bought multiple brands, the elder family members preferred Lifebuoy soap while the younger generation used the newer brands of toilet soap that were available in the market. The use of multiple brands is highest in the case of toilet soaps (see Table 4.1).

Table 4.1
Households using Multiple Brands

Category	Households (%)
Analgesics/cold/ethical tablets	27.6
Batteries	8.2
Biscuits	28.8
Bulbs	12.0
Digestives	11.6
Edible oils	15.4
Hairwash preparations	22.8
Rubs and Balms	10.1
Safety razor blades	16.1
Tea	26.0
Toilet soaps	42.9
Toothpowders	6.3
Toothpastes	8.6
Washing cakes/bars	30.7
Washing powders/liquids	21.9

Source: *Business World*, April, 1999.

In consumer non-durables, the need for a product variant is because of differing needs of consumers. These differences may be social, cultural or even variations within the family. The variations within the family are usually related to age and education (see Figure 4.2).

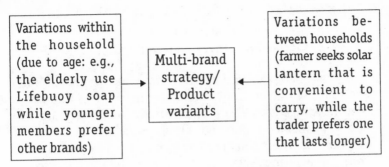

Figure 4.2 Variations Influencing Multi-brand Strategy

The preferences for durables also exhibit variations:

- Variations within a household are influenced by age: the type of watch preferred by a farmer would be different from that of his college-going son;
- Variations between households are also present:
  - the market for consumer durables is not only the land-owning farmers but also the non-agricultural occupation groups of shop keepers traders and those employed in service (government administration jobs, banks, teachers, other professionals etc.).
  - between the non-agricultural occupation groups, the service class seems to be far more fertile as a target group for higher end durables than the shopkeeper or trader (Bijapurkar and Murthy, 1992).

The type of products and their features preferred differ according to the occupation of the consumer. This could be influenced by perceptual and image factors or the differing use context. In a study of solar lanterns, it was found that farmers preferred lighter lanterns that could be easily carried, while traders sought lanterns that lasted for longer durations, as compared to consumers employed in service (see Box 4.1).

Box 4.1
Occupation Drives Preferred Features

The 'solar photovoltaic lantern' is a product promoted by the Ministry of Non-Conventional Energy Sources through state nodal agencies. These lanterns derive their energy from the solar radiation captured through solar modules fixed on rooftops. These solar modules are connected to the lantern and after the battery is charged can be disconnected for use as a portable lantern. During a study of rural consumers, it was found that farmers preferred to use the lantern for both indoor as well as outdoor use. An important feature in addition to the lighting quality and duration was the portability. Employees preferred to use it as an emergency lamp during power-cuts, especially during children's examinations. Traders used it in their shops during power-cuts and wherever power connections were not available. They preferred a longer duration lantern than either the employee or the farmer groups.

Consumer durable companies selling different products and their variants can therefore tailor their product offering and message according to the different usage pattern, targeting them for appropriate segments in the market.

Product Features and Positioning

Demonstrating the product is an effective way to educate and position the product in the consumer's mind. This method is used extensively to meet the challenge of:

- Generic competition;
- Brand competition.

Colgate–Palmolive uniquely competes with itself by promoting toothpaste in addition to toothpowder. The focus is on basic product and product education. It offers free samples and screens video films on oral hygiene. The Colgate advertisement of the wrestler with the weak tooth is targeted at users of charcoal powder and local toothpowder. It induces them to switch to Colgate toothpowder as the smooth white toothpowder has the ability to clean effectively without harming the teeth. The product features reinforce the positioning to help effectively compete against unbranded or low-priced local brands.

Education on the benefits of the product is common in rural markets. This is also seen in the case of shampoos. Shampoos are positioned as convenient, replacing the traditional soapnut or even soap in the rural market. A demonstration of product features and explaining product virtues is an approach used by some of the rural marketers. Hindustan Lever's campaign to wash shirts or shampoo the villagers hair free are instances of product education. In many such situations, potential consumers form queues to experience the product benefits.

Perception and Product Features

The perception of consumers in rural markets may vary. This has an important effect on product design and features (see Box 4.2).

Box 4.2
Product Design that Responds to Consumer Perceptions

Union Carbide found that its slick plastic torches, which were all the rage in the metros, had no takers in the villages. Farmers preferred heavy brass torches. Says Union Carbide managing director, V.P. Gokhale, 'With brass torches, they feel they are getting value for money'.

Texla drew a blank with its television sets that had grey and black cabinets, as farmers did not like sombre urban shades. It introduced a new range in bright red and yellow, which was reflected in a dramatically increased acceptance by the rural markets. (Das Gupta & Menon, 1990).

Philips primarily promotes the size of its music systems to rural consumers. Consumers are willing to pay a higher price for larger models, assuming that big is better. The company now makes its rural models one and a half times larger and louder than the ones for urban markets (Mukherjee, 1993).

The influence on perception of the rural consumer differ from that of the urban consumer. The size, shape, colour, hearing, smell and taste generate different set of response for the urban and the rural consumers. The product design and feature for rural markets need to reflect the consumer response to cues like size, shape etc.

Consumer needs dictate the generic product for both urban and rural markets. However, the *wants* of the consumer to meet a need may differ from a rural and an urban consumer. The product features sought by the rural market, therefore, may differ from the product features offered in the urban market.

Most pressure cookers are designed with handles on one side, which is fine if there is a controllable flame and the person cooking remains standing while preparing a meal, typical in an urban kitchen. The pressure cooker is, however, very unwieldy for use in the rural kitchen. A typical rural household uses an open fire or *chulha* with the person cooking squatting on the ground. The rural housewife may dream of some day owning a gas stove, but meanwhile she needs a wide-bodied cooker with handles on opposite sides.

Similarly, radios, cassette players and television sets are made to urban power supply specifications. In many villages, particularly in power-strapped states, voltages fluctuate wildly, making these products susceptible to frequent breakdowns. If products like the television or radio can withstand wide voltage fluctuations, consumers would not mind paying more for reliability. Efforts to develop products that suit the rural environment are:

- Cadbury's chocolates that do not melt so easily in the heat;
- LML's scooter with a more powerful engine aimed at the farmer which he can use for transporting goods (Das Gupta and Menon, 1990).

Environment factors, both physical and cultural, dictate consumer wants and therefore can provide the marketer with a basis for developing the product offering suited to the rural market.

Packaging

The decision on packaging is also influenced by the characteristics of the consumer. This includes:

- Affordability;
- Perceptions; and
- Ability to read.

Large groups of rural consumers receive daily wages and therefore have a limited amount of money to spend. These factors influence the size of the package preferred. An effective strategy in rural markets has been to sell products in smaller packs to suit smaller rural pockets. Hindustan Lever for instance introduced a smaller 75 gm. Lifebuoy soap and a 100 gm. Wheel detergent pack. The introduction of the shampoo sachet was a major packaging change that reflected the rural consumer's ability to spend. Godrej was one of the earliest companies to introduce the shampoo sachet of 6 ml, which cost Re. 1 (Joshi, 1991). The introduction of the sachet pack led to a boom in shampoo sales during the eighties. The sachet packaging was replicated in many other product categories. In the early nineties, Rasna Enterprises introduced a sachet for its soft drink concentrate. Priced at Rs. 5, the Rasna soft drink concentrate sachet makes six glasses (as compared to the regular pack, which costs Rs. 27.50 and makes 32 glasses) and is the main product in the company's rural marketing strategy (Ganguly, 2001).

The social and cultural variations in India's rural markets and prevailing literacy levels need to be understood for appropriate packaging decisions. As seen earlier, KMP Oils use packaging variations for different markets. This is also true for cigarettes. ITC sells its Goldflake brand with a yellow cover in the south, where it is associated with prosperity and purity. In the North, the package colour is golden as in this region yellow is often associated with jaundice and ill-health (Krishnamurthy, 1999).

The lower literacy levels enhance the need to exercise care in packaging decisions for rural markets. In the interior rural markets, brand identification is through visual patterns—a red soap cake signifies Lifebuoy soap. Distinct lettering, images or symbols that convey the product benefit also have an influence on consumer perceptions. A picture of lightning used with Rin detergent is distinct to the brand and its benefits and is easily identified by the illiterate consumer.

Pricing

The pricing issue is closely related to issues of positioning and packaging. As competition in rural markets is generally with the unorganised sector or against a product category, price is a critical factor in consumer choice. The presence of a very large price sensitive market does not mean the absence of rural consumers willing to pay a higher price for certain products or certain features.

It is not true that only cheap brands sell in rural markets. Usha found that the sale of its economy models were falling sharply in rural areas. Farmers prefer Usha's premier Century brand, though it is priced 20 percent higher (Das Gupta and Menon, 1990).

It is not necessarily a question of the relative price of brands as the actual purchase price or the money to be paid by the rural consumer. A landless labourer receives meagre daily wages and buys his provisions daily. He or she therefore buys something that has a small package price (see Box 4.3).

Box 4.3
Responses to Consumer Behaviour

Hindustan Lever found that retailers in villages were cutting its large 100 gm. Lifebuoy soap into smaller pieces and selling these. So it introduced a smaller 75 gm. pack. It also introduced Wheel detergent in a 100 gm. pack (Joshi, 1991).

Pricing should therefore be based on the ability to pay for all the necessities from the wages earned. The relative price of brands becomes secondary in this context. The farmer is willing to purchase higher priced brands when money is available, as he has surplus money after the harvest. This has important implications for product, pricing and promotion decisions. These decisions are clearly influenced by not just the income received but also on when it is received and how it is utilized. Pricing is therefore influenced by income stream and consumption.

This approach is referred to as *income stream and consumption basket pricing.* In contrast to the daily wage situation, the farmer has money after harvest, and may experiment with high-priced brands at this time. The price and positioning decision is therefore influenced not just by the income received but also on when it is received and how it is allocated among different needs.

Value—Not Price

Rural consumers look for value and not just price. Product strategy and pricing are closely linked to deliver value at the correct price. The success of the small shampoo sachet reflects the successful meeting of consumer needs. The high price of the cellular phone has been a barrier to widespread adoption even in urban areas. There is, however, acceptance in limited volumes in rural areas. Cellular phones help rural people to communicate long distance which otherwise is very difficult (see Box 4.4).

Box 4.4
Cellular Phone: Value for Money

An advertisement for cellular telephones now shows among others, a rural village merchant contacting the market to find out about prices and arrival of goods before he decides on purchase, stocking and despatch. The willingness to pay among consumers in the rural market has encouraged the cellular phone marketers to also target these consumers. The consumers innovate to add value and provide the marketers with opportunities for market development. The sachet concept is introduced by the consumers themselves for the cellular telephone when they share the bill for use of the cellular telephone. To tap the potential, Ushafone covers a number of villages with its cellular telephone service.

Product-sharing Service: Many rural consumers cannot afford high value durable products even though they have use for these products. Enterprising consumers cooperate to purchase the product and then share the service benefit. The alternative is the emergence of entrepreneurs who provide the 'product sharing service' as in the case of cellular telephones.

Value Offering: The marketer who succeeds is the one who constantly searches for ways and means to provide value to the consumer. This requires understanding the needs of the consumers and making an effort to meet these needs by offering a product that is affordable, like Usha International (see Box 4.5).

Box 4.5
Usha International Ltd.

Usha International Limited (UIL) of the Siddharth Shriram group proposes to increase its focus on the rural market, which contributes 50 percent of its total income. It plans to increase the penetration level of its fans in rural areas from the current five percent by introducing fans (both ceiling and table), designed to function under severe conditions of voltage fluctuations. They will be priced 30 percent less than normal. It also plans to increase the penetration level of its sewing machines in rural areas from the current 11 percent by introducing low cost models. UIL intends to route its products for the rural market through its diesel engine dealers, completing its strategy to make use of product design and pricing decision to deliver value to the rural consumer.

Decision Implications

Marketers can target consumers according to their unmet needs on price or product features and develop new markets through unique positioning.

The product and packaging are to be creatively used for developing and delivering value. The product attributes and features should reflect the environment of these consumers.

Marketers can use product and package design to influence perception. The size, shape and colour are important cues that a rural marketer can use to communicate effectively and create a favourable attitude. Distinct colours, designs and symbols help the illiterate rural consumer identify the brand. The ability to leverage strengths either in distribution or costs is important to deliver the value offering.

Value and not price is important in rural markets. It is relative value that is important, and so the launch price of a new product has to take into account the price of substitute products. In the case of non-essential items for which the consumer pays a large sum, demand for quality and preference for a brand name suggests offering a high-priced model in addition to offering a stripped down version. In the case of high-priced durables, the market potential can be enlarged through hiring the product. The presence of a large number of consumers has implications for package size of non-durables. It is preferable to have a small sachet with a low purchase price though priced higher than competing brands by unit of measure.

References

Bijapurkar, R. and Murthy, Ravi, 'Rural Markets for Consumer Durables' *The Economic Times*, August 16, 1999.

Business World, 'The Undiscovered Country', April 7–12, 1999.

Das Gupta, Surajeet and Menon, Ramesh, 'The Call of Consumerism', *India Today*, July 15, 1990.

Ganguly, Dibeyendu, 'Rasna flows straight into rural heart to boost SDC', *The Economic Times*, April 16, 2001.

Joshi, Anjali, 'The New El Dorado', *The Sunday Observer*, April 28–May 4, 1991.

Krishnamurthy, Narayan, 'Science speaks louder', *A&M*, November 30, 1999.

Mukherjee, Biman, 'The Fairground as Battlefield', *Business Today*, December 7–21, 1993.

FIVE

Communicating in the Rural Market Landscape

This chapter examines the complexity in communication strategies due to the spread and heterogeneity of rural markets. Managerial actions for reducing the large heterogeneous market into smaller homogenous ones are considered. A process perspective of communication is used to understand communication strategies in rural markets. The consumer influence on the communication process is examined to overcome the problem of selective comprehension. The influence of the stage of readiness and involvement of the consumer on communication is also discussed. These address the issue of selective comprehension by consumers. These different variables are put together by developing a taxonomy of communication strategies for rural markets.

Heterogeneity and Spread: A Challenge for Communication Strategies in Rural Markets

Communicating the message to rural consumers has posed enormous challenges to the rural marketer. One of the main problems is the large number of consumers scattered across the country. This problem is compounded as many of these consumers are not tuned in to the mass media. The second problem is the non-homogeneity of the market; although this factor is also an opportunity that the marketer can exploit for competitive advantage. Variations in the rural markets occur by geography, demography, selective perception or retention of individuals, the level of involvement in purchase behaviour and state of readiness.

Heterogeneity and spread has implications for decisions on media and message. The large spread of the rural markets and the limited reach of mass media impose limitations on universal communication to the rural consumer. Variations in language and culture also suggest a need for region-specific messages.

Managing Spread and Diversity

To grapple with the spread and enormous diversity in rural markets, it is necessary to reduce the situation to manageable proportions. This is done primarily through:

- Identifying geographical locations with a larger concentration of rural consumers;
- Locating potential consumers with a higher propensity to spend; and
- Localizing decisions on media and message using region specific budgets.

Going by the distribution of population in villages, it is apparent that a marketer need not reach out to every single village. In Uttar Pradesh, 27 percent of the villages account for 71 percent of the population. In other words, if 65 percent of the population needs to be covered in any state, it will be possible to do so by reaching out to a quarter or one-third of the villages (Bose, 1992).

There is a variation between villages and among the rural population in terms of the propensity to spend. It is therefore not necessary to reach out to 650 million people. A realistic figure would be a target group of 150 million rural adults with a propensity to spend.

Instead of a national release, the content and pattern of the advertising should be moulded to suit regional requirements. The promotion budget may be distributed amongst regional offices on the basis of past and expected sales volumes. This would then be utilized in conformity with local market conditions in different parts of the territory to create maximum synergy with sales efforts and distribution spread. Regional and area-wise operation of budgets enable carrying out product promotion in locations having a captive rural audience. *Haats* and *melas* present such opportunities.

Communication Strategies in Rural Markets

In rural markets the media used are diverse. The television route is used for the Nirma advertisement for detergents which are beamed to rural audiences and ONIDA's commercial on the magic of its black and white television. HLL uses a camel to advertise its detergents and Asian Paints demonstrates the effectiveness of their product on the horns of a bullock (Mukherjee, 1993). The information seeking and processing behaviour of the rural consumer influence the media and the message. The following messages indicate this—use of the moviestar Dharmendra to promote the Rajdoot motorcycle; one set of a Reckitt & Coleman commercial for Robin Blue does not use women.

To understand the influence on communication strategies and identify the critical influence on media and message decisions, a process perspective of communication is used.

Communication Process Perspective: The communication process model (see Figure 5.1) is used to understand some of the issues that need attention in media and message decisions.

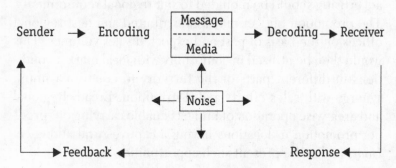

Figure 5.1 The Communication Process Model

The sender's task as can be seen from the model is to communicate the message to the receiver. The rural environment has a lot of influence on the receiver and therefore he or she may not receive the intended message for any of the following three reasons:

1. Selective attention: where the consumer may not notice the stimuli provided;
2. Selective distortion: where the message is twisted to hear what the consumer wants to hear; and
3. Selective recall: where the consumer permanently retains only a small fraction of the messages that reach him/her.

Comprehension of a message is therefore a critical problem in Indian rural markets. This is brought out in a study which tested the recall of messages sent using multiple media. The distortion of even illustrations in the study indicates the gravity of the problem (see Box 5.1).

Box 5.1
Selective Comprehension of Communication:
A Study of Farmers in Rajasthan

A study was carried out on the comprehension of communication near Udaipur. The media used were posters, film, leaflets and radio programmes. The message related to issues on rat control; spraying of a urea solution on wheat crop and poultry farming. From the response of a random sample of 80 farmers it was observed that the message was either not received or distorted. The drawing of a cyanide pump, for example, was taken to be a bicycle pump, and the rat was not understood to be dead. A beautifully made film about foliar, a fertilizer spray was wrongly understood as a process for pest control.

Consumer behaviour is a major influence on communication and therefore this influence is examined in the following section.

Consumer Behaviour Influence on Communication Strategies

The process of buying passes through different states of readiness of the buyer and this dictates the communication objectives. This includes a shift from a state of awareness to knowledge, then conviction, which results in purchase. The progress through the different state of readiness is moderated by the type of purchase (a new task or a repeat purchase) and also the level of involvement.

State of Readiness of the Consumer: This is observed during the purchase of a new product as compared to a new brand. The consumer first becomes aware of the product. He may or may not be convinced about the product. Once he is convinced, he purchases the product. At the time fertilisers were launched, the initial efforts were to create awareness, then interest followed by knowledge among potential consumers. The process of education was carried out by agricultural officers who educated farmers about fertilisers and explained their benefits. The conviction among consumers was created through demonstration. A demonstration in this case required the application of fertilisers in selective plots.

The risk for a consumer is relatively lower for a new brand as compared to a new product and therefore the consumer passes through the stages of awareness, knowledge and conviction much more quickly. The launch of the 25 HP tractor (255-DI) by Mahindra reflects this.

Their campaign took the consumer through each of the stages of awareness, interest, knowledge and conviction. The initial promotion was a teaser campaign informing the customers of an impending blue revolution. The next phase showed the tractor and its benefits were communicated using announcements, leaflets and banners. The third phase to create consumer conviction used direct personal contact with progressive farmers to explain the advantages and to demonstrate the tractor.

Involvement Level and Communication Strategies: The critical influences on consumer behaviour of 'level of involvement' and 'purchase experience' are used for classification of communication strategies in rural markets. The variation in communication strategies is mostly a reflection of consumer behaviour, his involvement and state of readiness. The involvement level of the buyer varies with different purchases. The involvement level is very high for high-risk items as in the purchase of a new consumer durable like a television. It is low for repurchase of a non-durable like salt. This is reflected in the manner in which the consumer seeks information. The effort on the part of the consumer to seek information is low when involvement levels are low and therefore there is a need to get the information to the consumer without much cost to him. In the case of a high involvement product, the consumer seeks information to reduce the risk of purchase and is willing to spend time and effort in making a purchase decision. The variation in the information seeking process of consumers is reflected in the communication strategies used by marketers. In rural markets, sewing machine is a high value, high involvement purchase. Usha International has started tailoring schools to educate and promote its sewing machines (Das Gupta and Menon, 1990). This is in contrast to the Nirma detergents (a non-durable) promotion through the television.

Taxonomy for Communication Strategies

Critical influences on consumer behaviour of the level of involvement and purchase experience are used for classification

Product Type	Stage in the Product Life Cycle		
	Introduction	Maturity	
		Brand Launch	Maintenance
Non-durable product	Use of demonstrations and trials to create knowledge and adoption	The focus is on creating an image and getting the retailer to promote	Reminder, advertisement and availability
Durables	Demonstration with focus on opinion, leaders to educate, create favourable attitude and conviction	Image building, demonstration of advantages and use of opinion leaders	Retaining image and customer satisfaction

Figure 5.2 Taxonomy for Communication Strategies

of communication strategies in rural markets. The level of involvement is reflected in the type of product and purchase experience captured by the stage in the product life cycle. Using concepts like 'type of product' and 'stage in the product life cycle' the following classification of 'communication strategies' is created (see Figure 5.2).

Communication Strategy by Situation

The communication strategy stage by stage in the product life cycle and by-product category are brought out in greater detail below.

1. Launch of a New Non-durable Product:
In the case of a new product, the consumer is not aware of the product and its usage. The marketer will find it relevant here to create an awareness of the product and induce its trial. Sampling and demonstrations are the methods used to educate the consumer. For instance, shampoo is promoted by demonstrating the application of shampoo. In the rural market it has been observed that during this kind of a demonstration, people queue up to have their hair shampooed. This method helps instruct the rural consumer in the use and benefits of shampoo, encouraging them to maintain clean and healthy hair. In certain cases it converted the consumer from the use of certain other products including bath soap. A similar approach was used for the launch of cigarettes (see Box 5.2).

Box 5.2
Launch of Cigarettes: The ITC Story

In 1910, when Imperial Tobacco introduced the cigarette in India, cigarette smoking was almost unknown as people smoked the native *chillums*, *hookahs* and *bidis*. For the early marketers waiting to convert the Indian rural market, selling was merely a question of gifting away thousands of cigarettes. The sales pitch was aimed at familiarising people with the unknown. A salesman's acumen was judged by the number of sticks he distributed. According to records, dispensing 50,000 to 100,000 cigarettes a month was considered to be a respectable number. The *modus operandi* was to hire a horse-drawn carriage from the nearest *bazaar* and cover it with gaily decorated placards advertising cigarettes. The vehicle travelled from district to district, with the district salesman and a section salesman sitting in full regalia showering cigarettes like so much confetti. While doing so, they would declaim the benefits of smoking. The more obvious venues—village *melas*—were singled out where a curious crowd would collect. Sometimes lucky dips and cigarette stalls were set up, with the more enterprising salesmen even organising lantern processions to popularise their brands. At these places, large groups would gather, most of whom had never seen a cigarette, let alone smoked one. The salesmen would demonstrate how to hold a cigarette in one's mouth, how to light it and how to smoke it.

These efforts at selling were backed by immature efforts at advertising. The publicity was mostly concentrated on such devices as posters, displays and promotional extravaganzas (Joshi, 1991).

2. Launch of a Non-durable Brand: In situations where a new brand is launched, the consumers are aware of the product. Loyalty to an existing brand among rural consumers is generally high. This requires creating awareness, image and trial for the brand. Mass media and non-conventional media is generally used for creating awareness and promoting brand benefits, while sampling is used to induce its trials. Efforts are also made to get the retailers to push the product. Nirma's advertisements which were simple and effective, helped entry into the rural markets near Jamshedpur. Regular servicing and attractive margins are the incentives for the channel members to promote new brands to consumers. HLL used a combination of mass media and better servicing of the rural retailer to promote its Wheel detergent (see Box 5.3).

Box 5.3
A Study on Consumer Response to Launch Strategies

In a study in rural markets near Jamshedpur, the consumer response to Nirma and Wheel strategies were examined. The survey indicated that Nirma was an early entrant. It entered the rural market without a strong distribution network, but because of its catchy advertising on television it was able to develop a demand-pull in the market. Wheels strategy launched subsequently also promoted the detergent as being easy on the hands. Wheel was distributed by field force. It succeeded in gaining entry and market share through better availability and creating a perception of quality (Velayudhan and Suri, 1996).

---

3. Communication for an Existing Non-durable Brand: The rural consumer is generally loyal to a brand and trial is through sales promotion or non-availability of an existing brand. A major focus of the marketer in this case is reminder advertising and sales promotion. Philips dresses up people to look like its bulbs and batteries and parades them through the villages. As availability is important in addition to reminder advertising, servicing the rural retailer is critical. Colgate–Palmolive has supply vans to service the retailer and it also uses the vans for promotion. It offers free samples and screens video films on oral hygiene during these visits.

4. Launch of a New Durable: The rural consumer first becomes aware of the product during the launch of a durable. Interest is generated in the product when he/she hears neighbours and friends discuss the new product. He/she then learns more about the product and then on the advice of others, decides on its purchase. The decision to purchase the product and its model and type is made by the consumer after deliberating with the retailer and other users. Demonstrations to create awareness and knowledge and identifying opinion leaders for focussed communication are critical in such situations. Arvind Mills promoted its 'Ruf and Tuf' jeans to rural markets. Its promotion effort included teaching tailors in villages to stitch the jeans. The tailors who are the opinion leaders for clothing become votaries for jeans and for the 'Ruf and Tuf' brand (Ghosh and Krishnaswamy, 1997).

In certain situations, where trial of the product is not possible, opportunities to use it free of cost is arranged for the consumers. Usha International, manufacturers of sewing machines ran sewing schools in villages which offered short-term tailoring courses for women. This creates excitement around the product and demonstrates its utility. It educates the consumer on its use and builds confidence with potential buyers. The demonstration method and opinion influencers is seen in the promotion of the smokeless *chulha*.

5. Launch of a Durable Brand: A consumer interested in a particular product looks for different options and seeks opinion from dealers and existing users. He/she is also interested in seeing demonstrations of the product. The marketer needs to invest time and effort to break into such a market. The product needs to have a demonstrable advantage over other competitive products. The brand can be made popular by promoting to key persons in the village who become ambassadors for the brand. Hindustan Motors demonstrates the utilities of its vehicle on the dirt tracks to rural consumers (Ghosh and Krishnaswamy, 1997). The launch of the new 25

HP tractor by Mahindra creates brand acceptance in the consumer through awareness, interest, knowledge and persuasion (see Box 5.4).

Box 5.4
Launch of a New Tractor Model

Mahindra & Mahindra launched its new 25 HP tractor model—Mahindra 255-DI in blue (all its other tractors are red). Haryana was the choice for the campaign because of the large concentration of 25 HP tractors and the strong presence of lower-end buyers in this state. The first three phases of the campaign were unleashed over three weeks that began January, 1999. Phase one began with a teaser campaign, warning the farmers of an impending blue revolution, without revealing the product or the company. This exercise covered 200 villages around seven key dealerships in Haryana. The objective was to create curiosity and entertainment among rural folk, and urge them to look forward to the next phase.

Phase two saw an election convoy introducing the tractor for the first time. The idea at this point was to show the product and to communicate its benefits via jingles, announcement, leaflets and banners.

The next phase saw the formal launch ceremonies for which personalised invitations were sent to key customers in every village. Working demonstrations were used to show the superiority of the tractor. Farmers were allowed to test it out on their lands.

---

6. Communication for an Existing Durable Brand: The rural consumer may want to buy a durable for the first time or replace an existing one. He/she looks for alternatives from existing users and experts before making the purchase. Performance of the existing brand is an important criterion for the consumer who is already using the product and keen to replace it. Loyalty is high if the consumer is satisfied with the existing brand. In this situation it is important for the marketer to maintain the image and ensure customer satisfaction. It is necessary to communicate the advantages of the brand with existing and potential customers over its rivals. It is necessary for existing customers to perceive that their choice of brand is correct. Communication to potential customers who have not used the brand can be from existing users or through the media. The communication objective is to get the consumer to perceive this brand as good. Onida advertises the magic of its black and white television. Eicher highlights the fuel efficiency of its tractors. It also demonstrates its superiority over other brands through a contest (see Box 5.5).

Box 5.5
Pulling Ahead: Demonstrating the Superiority of a Brand

The marketing team at Eicher Tractors supplements its copious literature on fuel-efficiency with the emotional route to appeal to rural consumers. Eicher organizes tug-of-war contests between its own tractors and those of rival companies at the colourful Pushkar fair in Rajasthan. As the audience cheers, the Eicher Tractor wins the contest (Mukherjee, 1993).

Decision Implications

A marketer has to identify region specific media and develop regional messages. This is to be implemented by developing region and area-wise budget for promotion. A marketer also needs to research the audience state of readiness and information search behaviour for their products for effective promotion.

The launch of a new non-durable into the market can use demonstration and sampling to educate the consumer and create conviction. Demonstration and sampling for a new brand helps to create brand awareness and pushes the product through the channel. The marketer of an existing non-durable brand can use reminder advertising and sales promotion to retain the loyalty of the rural consumer. The launch of a new durable will use demonstration for creating awareness and to generate a favourable attitude among opinion leaders. In the case of a new brand of a durable product the demonstration helps create advocates among experts. The existing brand of durable has to ensure customer satisfaction for getting advocates from customers.

References

Bose, D. K., 'Reaching out to the Rural Millions', *Brand Equity, The Economic Times*, October 28, 1992.

Das Gupta, Surajeet and Menon, Ramesh, 'The Call of Consumerism', *India Today*, July 15, 1990.

Ghosh, Joydeep and Krishnaswamy, Chetan, 'The Rural Rush', *The Week*, October 19, 1997.

Joshi, Anjali, 'Rural Markets: The New El Dorado', *The Sunday Observer*, April 28–May 4, 1991.

Mukherjee, Biman, 'The Fairground of Battlefield', *Business Today*, December 7–21, 1993.

Velayudhan, Sanal Kumar and Suri, B., 'Rural Market Response - A Tentative Study', *Management and Labour Studies*, Vol. 21, No. 1., 1996.

SIX

Communication: Language and Culture

This chapter looks at the rural consumers' receptivity to the advertising message. The factors that affect the message effectiveness is identified. The meaning derived from a message is from the language. Variations in the complexity of the language influences the effectiveness of the message. Pictorial presentations are examined for effectiveness among rural and urban consumers. The utilitarian and narrative forms of the message are examined. Characteristics of trustworthiness, likeability, expertise and situational associations are examined for the nature of the impact they have on the rural consumers.

Receptive Rural Consumers

In a study on the perceived influence of advertising, it was observed that rural consumers considered advertising in a more positive light than urban consumers. Rural consumers perceived the influence of advertising to buy 'products they do not need' to be much less as compared to the same perception among urban consumers. Again fewer rural consumers perceive the advertisements to be misleading (see Box 6.1).

Box 6.1
The Perceived Influence of Advertising

The National Council for Applied Economic Research (NCAER) conducted a survey sponsored by the Indian Society of Advertisers on 'Socio-economic effects of Advertising'. The survey covered 3,836 households in 50 towns and 50 rural districts in 10 states, showing a clear rural–urban divide. Sixteen percent of rural respondents felt that advertising influenced them to frequently or always buy products they do not really need; the corresponding figure for urban respondents was 25 percent. Nineteen percent of the rural respondents felt that advertisements are frequently misleading while 30 percent of the urban respondents thought so (Shirali, 1993).

Message Effectiveness

A number of factors affect the effectiveness of a message. The message for the rural market has to reflect the framework that is meaningful to the rural consumer. This suggests that message decisions need to take into account the following aspects for their effectiveness (see Figure 6.1).

- **Language:** The message has to be understood. This requires communicating in a language that is meaningful to the consumer. This suggests:
  – a message that is simple
  – the use of appropriate words
- **Pictorial Presentation:** The use of visuals as part of the message is important in rural markets as literacy levels are low. This includes:
  – use of pictures and colours
  – use of symbols, including logos
- **Message form:** The effective communication to rural consumers should be:

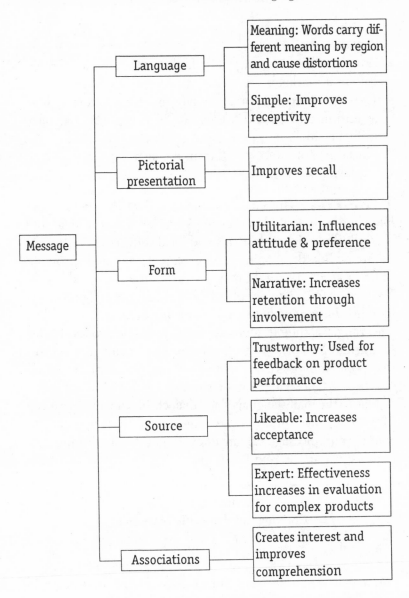

Figure 6.1 Message Decisions

- utilitarian
- narrative
- **Source of the Message:** Credibility of the source is critical for rural markets.
- **Context Association:** Associations create interest, hold attention and provide meaning. The aspects that have influence include:
  - products of interest to the rural consumer
  - relevant settings

Language: The message should reflect the culture and language of the rural audience. A marketer has to take into account the religion, festivals and local sentiments of the rural area while developing the message. Companies promote their products in rural areas that are based on rural tastes. Dabur has found it very effective to distribute religious texts like the *Hanuman chalisa* and *Ramcharitmanas* or calendars with religious themes along with its ayurvedic products (Das Gupta and Menon, 1990). A soil conditioner called Terracare uses popular figures from mythology images to attract the rural consumer (Ghosh and Krishnaswamy, 1997).

Due to the many languages and dialects in our country, words sometimes have different meanings in different parts of the country and message effectiveness depends on tailoring it to regional variations (see Box 6.2).

Box 6.2
Creating Rural-specific Messages

Not all commercials are accepted by rural folk. Social workers recount stories of advertisements that confuse or scandalize rural viewers. For instance, members of some rural communities in Rajasthan were offended by the Halo shampoo spot featuring female models with beautiful, bouncy hair. The reason was that here it is considered indecent for women to let down their hair in public. The same villagers were bemused by the Strepsils *Bahut Mazaa Aya* advertisement. In their dialect, the word *mazaa* has a strong sexual connotation, and they could not understand how anyone could get corporeal pleasure from a cough lozenge. (Ghosh, 1994)

A Simple Presentation: What appeals to the rural audience is a simple message. Presentations should therefore be simple, comprehensible and in a language understood by the rural consumer (see Box 6.3).

Box 6.3
Complex Communication as Barriers to Reception

It is relevant to share our recent experience on a market survey on pesticides. Here we have a serious communication problem. Though there are local names of pests, but all the material released by all the pesticides companies mostly identify the pests by their English and academic nomenclature. There are generic names used for pesticides which again are in English. Some of these names are difficult to pronounce e.g., monocrotophos, the brand name such as Nuvacron. The choice for the consumers increases in complexity because of additional dimensions. Additional dimensions are the manufacturers, formulation strength, product form and varying percentages of technical material content.

The entire exercise is so complicated that the marketing organisations are not able to effectively communicate with the farmer on the brand name of the pesticide for a given pest. The result is not only an improper and wrong selection of pesticide but also that the recommended dosages are not being used, and the farmer blames the pesticide and the manufacturer for the ineffective treatment. The fertiliser people have introduced simple symbols and brands like Star brand, Crescent brand etc. Some such sign language needs to be developed in case of pesticides (Jain, 1983).

Pictorial Presentation: Visual messages appeal the most to rural audiences. For instance, motorbikes that picturise a cheetah or a stallion to convey speed have universal appeal. A study on the recall of pictorial advertisements as compared to non-pictorial advertisements indicate how much more effective they are with rural consumers as compared to urban consumers (see Box 6.4).

Box 6.4
Study on the Effectiveness of Pictorial Advertisements

In a study in West Bengal, four of the eight advertisements shown to respondents were classified as pictorial. The percentage of pictorial advertisements from among those recalled by the respondent were used as the measure of effectiveness of pictorial advertisements.

Results of the Recall Test

Percentage of pictorial advertisements within total recall				
Rural	< 25%	26–50%	51–75%	> 75%
Number of respondents	8	38	8	6
Percentage	133	633	133	10
Urban				
Number of respondents	25	24	6	2
Percentage	41.6	40	10	3

Sixty three percent of the respondents recalled between 26 to 50 percent of pictorial advertisements while 13 percent recalled less than 25 percent. Forty one percent of urban respondents recalled less than 25 percent of pictorial advertisements. This indicated that a larger number of respondents in rural markets had a higher percentage recall of pictorial advertisements as compared to respondents in urban areas (Das, 1994).

Visual Message and Positioning: The rural consumer is influenced by language, signs, symbols and pictorial
presentations. As discussed in Chapter 4, the design of the
product, the packaging, including the size, shape and colour
help create a strong image in the mind of the rural consumer.
The savvy marketer uses signs and symbols the villager can
identify with to successfully promote his product. In rural markets, visual messaging and positioning are important tools that
no marketer can afford to overlook (see Box 6.5).

Box 6.5
Signs and Symbols in Rural Markets

A number of successful brands in rural markets have brand
names or symbols with numbers or animals. These include:
555 soap, Monkey brand toothpowder, Gemini tea (with
an elephant), Cheetah fight matches or 'Sheeru' (tiger) *beedi*
and Tiger cigarettes. The association of symbols with these
brands help recollection. The 3–Roses brand of tea makes
the rural consumer 'think and feel fresh'. The symbol helps
associate the product features with the brand of tea. The
symbols that make the consumer feel and think about features that are relevant for the product are critical for brand
building in the rural market (Krishnamurthy, 1999).

Utilitarian Message: Rural consumers prefer utilitarian messages that link benefit to product attribute over value
expressive advertisements. A study was carried out to test the
effectiveness of utilitarian messages in an advertisement for a
detergent bar of soap which promised extra whiteness through
extra foam. The second advertisement showed a mother and
child in dazzling white clothes asking the viewer whether he/
she used the detergent bar like they did. Sixty three percent of
the respondents from the rural market preferred the brand
which promised extra whiteness through extra foam.

The number of claims to use in an advertisement is also an important decision variable for the marketer. Multiple Claims in a message appear to create favourable attitudes though viewers do not necessarily comprehend all claims (see Box 6.6).

Box 6.6
Message Characteristics

In a study covering three villages in West Bengal the characteristics of messages were studied by showing advertisements. The advertisements were created for non-existent brand names in the product categories studied. The product categories studied were soaps, detergent cakes, mosquito repellent coils, bicycles and motorbikes.

Messages for mosquito repellent coils with a single claim of 'delivering a good night's sleep', and another with multiple claims like it 'drives away flies, mosquitoes and spreads pleasant perfume', were exposed to respondents. Though only 40 percent of the respondents could recall all the claims made in the multiple claims advertisement, 90 percent of the respondents preferred the brand supported with multiple claims (Das, 1994).

Narrative Message: The use of stories for promotion of products to rural consumers is common with marketers. Colgate–Palmolive and HLL have story-based commercials running for over 20 minutes. Castrol has a movie with the brand names of lubricants portrayed as characters in the movie.

Message Source: Three types of message sources are identified:

- A likeable source;
- A trustworthy source; and
- An expert source.

1. Likeable source: Testimonial advertising using film stars have also been quite successful though mostly for non-durables as in the case of Lux soap. However, this has been used even for durables. Rajdoot motorcycle sales dipped from 85, 000 to 76, 000 units in 1987. Rajdoot was perceived as being rugged, easily manoeuvrable on rural tracks and having the ability to carry loads. To capitalise the growing rural segment, Rajdoot used Dharmendra who represented the 'son of the soil' image. This advertisement resulted in sales crossing 1,00,000 pieces in 1990 (Rajan, 1992).

2. Trustworthy source: Rural markets depend upon word-of-mouth communication to a large extent. The villager prefers to use a source on whom he/she can trust; these are generally friends, relatives or neighbours. In a study on influences upon consumer behaviour in villages near Jamshedpur, it was observed that the most important interpersonal source was the person who possessed the product. (Sirbhaiya, 1993). This is because it is considered a trustworthy source.

3. Expert source: In a study, for the purchase of durables, opinion leaders were consulted to find out more about the product. Opinion leaders were defined according to product category. For example a *mistry* (mechanic) was considered the person to be consulted in the case of bicycles and a tailor in the case of sewing machines (Sirbhaiya, 1993). The importance of expert opinion is observed from a study in the villages of West Bengal (see Box 6.7).

Box 6.7
The Influence of Source Characteristics
on Purchase of Motorcycles

The credibility of a source is more important in rural markets than the attractivness of a source. This was observed in a study where 60 respondents from three villages were

---

exposed to two advertisements for motorcycles. One of the advertisements was recommended by Kapil Dev and another by an engineer. Sixty seven percent of the respondents preferred the brand endorsed by the engineer and one-third of them explicitly stated 'recommended by the engineer' as the reason for this preference (Das, 1994).

Context Associations

Products of Interest to the Consumer: The recall of advertisements on products of relevance to rural audiences was higher when compared with the recall for the same products by urban consumers. This was observed in a study by NCAER on the 'socio-economic effects of advertising'. In this study it was observed that the recall of advertisements was generally higher in urban areas. It, however, varied between urban and rural audiences depending on product usage. For example, fertiliser and pesticide advertisements had far higher recall in rural areas.

Relevant Environment or Situation: The rural audience is influenced by the context of the advertisement. Advertisements with urban settings or those that are far removed from their everyday life do not find favour as they are unable to relate to such a presentation. The rural consumer is, therefore, not influenced by advertisements that depict a different world, as he/she finds these advertisements difficult to comprehend (see Box 6.8).

Box 6.8
Context in Advertisements

Advertisements showing a different world, which viewers do not comprehend are ineffective. This was observed when an advertisement for bicycles showed young men and women dressed in trendy, urban outfits. This was an advertisement for a brand that the respondents were not aware of. The other advertisement was a freshly developed one about a non-existent brand. The visual and the copy linked the cycle with the mirth and merriment of the *Durga Puja*. Seventy percent of the respondents from rural locations liked and understood the *Durga Puja* advertisement, while only 23 percent of the respondents understood the advertisement of the trendily dressed young men and women. Similarly 70 percent of the respondents preferred the brand advertisement that portrayed the *Durga Puja* over the other brand (Das, 1994).

Decision Implications

Messages targeted at the rural consumer need to be simple, comprehensible and in a language understood by the consumer. The use of pictures adds to the effectiveness. Narratives that use stories increase the retention of the message.

Content of the message, too, needs attention. A message that associates a benefit with a product attribute is effective. Multiple claims are effective in rural markets as compared to urban markets. A message that highlights the relevance of the product creates interest and better recall.

The content and source of communication is important for the rural market. Advertisements need to use settings that are familiar to the rural consumers. The rural consumer also seeks the opinion of relevant others. Educating, training and incentivising the opinion leaders increase acceptance among consumers. Communicating and satisfying existing users or consumers is an effective way of generating a favourable word-of-mouth. Use of testimonials from film stars are also effective.

References

Das Gupta, Surajeet and Menon, Ramesh, 'Rural Markets: The Call of Consumerism', *India Today*, July 15, 1990.

Das, Sandeep, 'Advertising in Rural Markets: Message Effectiveness'. An unpublished report submitted as part of PGDBM course, XLRI, Jamshedpur, 1994.

Ghosh, Aparisim, 'The New Rules of Rural Marketing', *Business World*, April 6–19, 1994.

Ghosh, Joydeep and Krishnaswamy, Chetan, 'The Rural Rush', *The Week*, Vol. 15, No. 44, 1997.

Jain, B.K.S. 'Technical note for the Agricultural Import Marketing Course', IIM, Ahmedabad, November, 1983.

Krishnamurthy, Narayan, 'Signs Speak Louder', *A&M*, November 30, 1999.

Rajan, Ravi, 'Hooking on to a new channel', *Brand Equity, The Economic Times*, August 12, 1992.

Shirali, Aresh, 'A Matter of Perceptions', *A&M*, February, 1993.

Sirbhaiya, Anupam, 'The Role of Mass Media and Interpersonal Communication as a Source of Information for the Rural Consumer'. An unpublished report submitted as part of PGDBM course, XLRI, Jamshedpur.

SEVEN

Operationalising Communication Strategy: Issues and Approaches in Media

This chapter looks at the reach of media in rural markets in comparison with the reach of media in urban markets. Influence of audience profiles and behaviour on the effectiveness of media is examined. For different media the recall and attitude change is observed to identify media effectiveness. The impact of non-conventional media in rural markets is seen to be high. Their ability to create awareness, knowledge, attitude change and persuasion is also examined. The emerging non conventional media of audio visual vans and point-of-purchase channels are examined in some depth.

Media Reach

The reach of terrestrial television and satellite television is less in rural areas compared to urban areas, although it has the largest reach compared to other media, like the press or radio (see Figure 7.1) Television is popular with an increasing number of the rural population. Almost half the rural population can be reached by the total mass media i.e., (television, press, radio and cinema).

The reach of television has remained constant from 1997 to 1999; the growth observed mostly due to satellite television. This phenomenon has increased the reach in certain rural areas in south India, coastal areas of Andhra Pradesh, Tamil Nadu and Kerala. Terrestrial television has 36 percent penetration in households while satellite television has a limited penetration. The advantage of this media is that it has the lowest cost per thousand and is therefore attractive to fast moving consumer goods (FMCG). The absence of a focus on consumer segments and the non-separation of urban and rural audiences are the major drawbacks of the television medium.

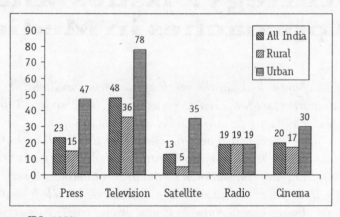

Source : IRS, 1999.
Media reach figures are based on the following parameters:
Cinema : at least once in three months
Press : average readership per issue
Terrestrial T.V., Satellite TV and Radio : at least once a week

Figure 7.1 Overall Media Reach

Radio has both an urban and rural audience. F.M. and Vividh Bharti have urban listeners but primary radio channels have semi-urban and rural audiences. There are 173 such stations. The rates are according to those announced by the government.

The press has a limited reach in most rural areas. The exception is in Kerala where it is 65 percent.

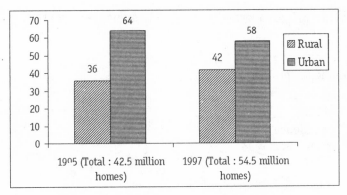

Source: Ray (1998).

**Figure 7.2 Distribution of Television
in Rural and Urban Homes**

The use of outdoor media is very relevant for rural areas. Options available to marketers include wall paintings, posters, the use of space on hand pumps for water, hoardings etc. However this is expensive and has a restricted reach. There is also no benchmark for pricing, and quality usually suffers in the bargain for rates.

Factors that Influence Media Effectiveness

For a marketer, the reach of the media and its effectiveness are important. The factors that affect media effectiveness and the audience response to different media are examined (see Figure 7.3).

A number of factors affect media effectiveness. These include:

- Audience profile;
- Media preferences;
- Channel and programmes viewed; and
- Audience behaviour.

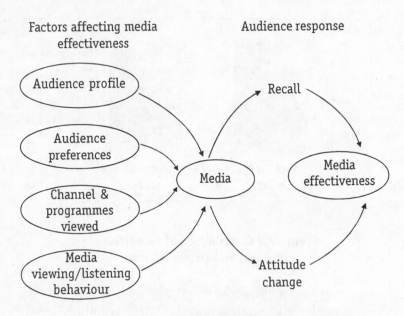

Factors affecting media
effectiveness

Audience response

Figure 7.3 Media Effectiveness

Audience Profile: Upmarket rural audiences are exposed to mass media. A large section of the rural upmarket audience can be reached by television alone (see Table 7.1).

Table 7.1
Reach of Mass Media by Income Group

(Percentages)

Media	MHI* Rs 5,000+	MHI Rs. 3,001– Rs 5,000	MHI < Rs 3,000	All
T.V.	59	63	30	33
T.V. & Radio	68	74	40	44
T.V. + Radio + Press	73	80	46	49
T.V. + Radio + Press + Cinema	74	80	48	51

*MHI - monthly household income
Source IRS, 1998, Sarkar, (1998).

Young male members are the majority viewers of television (Das and Sen 1991).

Media Preferences: It has been recognised that the effectiveness of media depends largely on the audience. As observed earlier, consumers in the higher income category have access to mass media and are more receptive to it. Traditional media are likely to be more effective with the average rural audience which is less cosmopolitan and have a lower income. In a study on communication of health information to rural people, the media channels were ranked on effectiveness. Interpersonal communication was ranked the most effective followed by television/VCR, print and then radio (Chandra, 1992).

Channel and Programmes Viewed: It has been observed that the rural viewer does not switch channels. Brand loyalty to a programme is fairly high. This is influenced by the presence of a large number of black and white televisions and lower priced colour televisions that have limited channels. DD1 is the channel with the highest viewership. For mass products, popular network programmes can be used to the marketers' advantage. The cost per thousand contacted works out to as low as one rupee. The viewership patterns of the popularly watched programmes on Doordarshan help illustrate this (see Table 7.2).

Table 7.2
Viewership Patterns On DD–1

(in millions)

Programme	Urban	Rural	Total
Rangoli	52	42	94
Hindi films	59	57	116

Programmes that are popular in urban areas are also popular among rural audiences, though it has been observed that a large group does not fully comprehend the main theme. A fairly large section of the audience feels that advertisements are not related to their world and do not view them favourably. This is observed in a study covering multiple locations (see Box 7.1).

Box 7.1
Audience Response to Television Commercials

A study on audience response to television commercials was conducted in Purulia (West Bengal), Erode (Tamil Nadu), and Kheda (Gujarat). Its findings were:

- People below the age of 35 years watch more television. Around 70 to 80 percent were males, 30 to 40 percent were illiterate and the majority were farmers or farm labourers.
- More than 60 percent of viewers watch national programmes
- In the South and North, films and musical programmes like *Chitrahaar* are viewed but news programmes are more popular in the South
- Around 60 percent understand the main theme, 10 to 20 percent remember only the visuals and do not comprehend the meaning, while only 12 percent understand the words. Programmes in English are understood by a minority
- Around 26 percent do not like advertisement slots between programmes while 70 percent like them. Those who dislike advertisements feel that visuals mostly show a different world and are not able to identify with them.
- In Purulia, 15 percent consider attire depicted vulgar while in Erode 10 percent consider it vulgar
- Regarding toiletry items, more than television exposure, the proximity to urban areas was a stronger factor in changing rural habits. Television did however assist trials in affordable brands (Das and Sen, 1991).

Audience Behaviour: Audience behaviour is examined for important media like television, radio and newspaper as their behaviour influences media decisions.

Television Viewing Behaviour

Media decisions are guided by viewing habits. Television in rural markets means Doordarshan. Since the rural routine is not as dominated by the clock as the case in urban areas, a prime time television programme may mean that the viewer switches on the set 20 to 30 minutes earlier. Typically, about 10 minutes before prime time there is a switch over to the national network. Advertising rates before this happens are relatively low and could bring in the same kind of mileage as prime time advertising does.

Radio Listening

Radio is a popular media. Besides AIR's primary channel programmes, Vividh Bharati is also heard regularly. It is not only farm news and Samachar but film music that is popular. This is because rural consumers listen in to the radio throughout the day, unlike in urban India where people listen to the radio in the mornings. The sponsor has to exercise care in the media and its usage as otherwise the message is unlikely to be heard among the target audience. For instance, a tractor jingle at 11.00 p.m. hardly has a rural audience and is of little advantage to the advertiser.

Access to Newspapers

Newspapers normally reach the feeder market or small towns, and are read in shops or roadside hotels. People sometimes buy newspapers here and take them back home where they are read by other people. In some cases the newspaper is read at the common gathering/meeting. Social gatherings or friendly get-togethers differ from village to village. In Nayadih village near Jamshedpur, the mosque was a common meeting place in the evening or after prayers. The younger generation also frequently meets in the evening (Sirbhaiya, 1994).

Audience Response to Media

Audience response to different media is examined for awareness, knowledge and influence. Awareness and knowledge is measured through recall and influence measured through attitude, which is what the consumer goes through before purchase decision.

Recall by Media: A study was carried out in 50 towns and 50 rural districts covering 3,836 households on advertising recall. A comparison showed that the recall of advertisements was generally higher in the urban areas, except in the case of radio. In this case, the recall was higher in rural areas (see Figure 7.4). It is possible that the results are influenced by the sample and also by the measures used. The

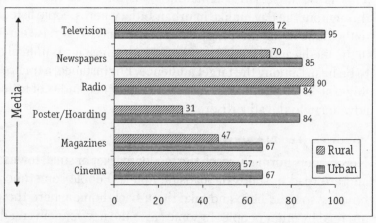

Source: Shirali, 1993.   (all figures are in percentages)

Figure 7.4 Recall of Advertising by Media

measures used to indicate advertising recall were generalised questions and not responses to specific advertisements. If we ignore the possible influence of methodology on the results, it shows that variations exist on media effectiveness between rural and urban markets. Recall is not necessarily low in rural areas for all media.

Influence on Attitude: The communication objective of attitude changes and inducing preferences is more effectively performed through an interpersonal approach. It was observed in a study that more than television exposure, the proximity to urban areas was a stronger factor in changing rural habits (Das and Sen, 1991). The influence of rural retailers on attitudes and preferences is brought out in two studies (see Box 7.2).

Box 7.2
The Rural Consumer Lends an Ear to the Retailer

Two studies suggest the influence of the retailer on the rural consumer:

- In a study that compared urban consumers in Calcutta and rural consumers from three villages in West Bengal, it was observed that retailers are the major influence in purchase of soaps. In the urban areas, 'advertisements' influenced attitudes, of which television was the dominant media (Das, 1995).
- A study on the role and influence of the retailer was carried out in East Singhbum, a district of Bihar. In this study, the rural areas included the Haata and Kaandra villages, situated about 25 kms from Jamshedpur. The urban centre for the study was the city of Jamshedpur. The study suggests that the importance of the rural retailer as a source of information is greater for the rural consumer than for the urban consumer (Baptist, 1992).

It is not only the retailer but traditional media (*kavi sammelan*, puppet shows, etc.) that hold sway over the rural audience. This is because the effectiveness of media depends upon the audience. Traditional media has a greater impact on motivational, behavioural or attitudinal aspects of rural people, while mass media is effective in the quick transmission of information and news. The traditional media enjoys acceptability and credibility. Rural drama meets all intellectual, emotional and aesthetic needs of the villagers.

Non-conventional Media

Non-conventional media is seen to be effective among the rural audience. A number of non-conventional media are available, some of which are wall paintings, audio-visual vans and demonstration and sampling (see Box 7.3).

Box 7.3
Non-conventional Media

Local promotional activities could include:
– wall paintings
– direct mail
– banners placed on elephants parading through main bazaars
– puppetry
– processions, tableaus, floats, etc.
– contests to promote the products
– audio visual vans
– stalls, hoardings and audio-visual publicity at local fairs
– point-of-purchase channels
– demonstrations and sampling at *haats* and fairs

The effectiveness of these media vary. Different media can be utilised for achieving different communication objectives.

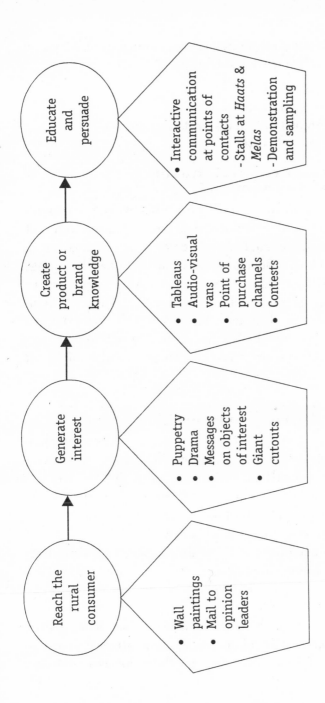

Figure 7.5 : Communicating Using Non-conventinal Media

Non-conventional media are examined from the following communication objectives (see Figure 7.5).

- Reach;
- Ability to generate interest;
- Create product or brand knowledge; and
- Educate and persuade

Media for Effective Reach of Rural Consumers

Wall paintings and direct mail are an effective way to communicate to the rural consumer. Wall paintings present a cost-effective option but are limited to creating only a visual impact as literacy is low. Nirma makes extensive use of wall paintings.

A mailing campaign can be very useful with opinion leaders, influencing agencies and agents of change. The copy should be brief but well illustrated. The mailing lists can comprise tractor owners. The mailing list is relevant not only for agricultural inputs but also consumer durables and even certain non-durables.

Media that Generates Interest in the Audience

A media that generates interest among the audience is important to overcome selective attention. The use of a novel media or media that stands out and compels attention are useful to generate awareness and brand name retention. Such media may include puppetry or drama and putting messages on objects that interests the rural audience.

Fertiliser manufacturer BASF uses puppetry to convey their messages. Even simple tales gain from the colour and enchantment of the medium. The medium of the message helps in attracting attention.

This occurs when the target audience notices it in activities and situations that are of interest to them. Messages on camels, horses, and elephants during exhibitions and fairs have proved to be an effective medium. It is not only the animals or animate objects that interest the rural audience. Instead of staid bill boards or giant cut-outs, putting the message on objects of interest during events can be effective in attracting attention and creating brand awareness and brand recall (see Box 7.4).

Box 7.4
Capturing the Attention of Rural Consumers

A. Messages on animals
   This is hard sell in the hinterland. Under a mild winter sun, colours whirl, bodies jostle, and the sand flies as the camel race, most revered ritual at the Pushkar *Mela* in Rajasthan begins. Frenzied spectators line the route of the race, waiting for their hump-backed champions to be flagged off.
   As the starter's whistle sounds and a roar of anticipation goes up, the front-runners break out of the pack, their hooves thundering, the sound mingling with the cheers from the crowd. All eyes are drawn to the leaders, each displaying its colour proudly: the blue and green of Rin and Wheel detergents from Hindustan Lever Ltd (HLL), the blue of Panacur and Butox pills from Hoechst and the white of H. B., a strong veterinary medicine from Indian Herbs.

B. Messages on objects
   – HLL used to station a giant Lifebuoy boat at Alwaye, during the annual Onam festival's boat race in Kerala
   – Colgate–Palmolive used to splash its name on kites during Gujarat's kite festival
   – SPIC would sponsor bull fights in Tamil Nadu (Mukherjee, 1993).

Media to Create Product or Brand Knowledge

Novel and exciting media that brings out the advantages of the product or brand are used by marketers. These include processions and tableaus, contests, audio-visual vans and point-of-purchase channels.

Excitement-oriented activities such as processions, tableaus, floats, etc. are common place in rural markets, e.g., HLL dressing up a propagandist as 'Superman' to demonstrate the superwashing power of Rin. In rural towns, such promotional activities are vital to create and build awareness about the product and communicate its message.

Contests involving products and the consumers themselves are used to create awareness and brand recall. These contests result in brand recall because of the high level of involvement they generate among the participants. Philips organises shouting matches. The person who can shout Philips name the loudest wins. The contest makes a clear association between the company's audio equipment and loudness (Mukherjee, 1993).

Audio-visual vans and point-of-purchase are the emerging non-conventional media that are used to create product or brand knowledge. These have emerged as important methods to reach the rural audience and are treated separately.

Educating and Persuading the Rural Consumer

Interactive media, demonstration and sampling are used in order to educate and persuade the rural consumer.

Interactive Media: Communication can be informative and bring about attitude change. This is possible when the media generates interaction through participation and involvement of the target audience. Some of the points of contact with the audience can be during fairs and festivals, *haats*, *mandis*, folk performances, and at other special events at banks, post offices, schools, and village wells etc. An important point of interaction is at sugar mills. During the cane-crushing season, hordes of rural decision makers congregate at sugar mills with their crop. These points of contact provide opportunities for interactive communication. Some of the media indicated earlier are amenable for interactive communication. The audio-visual vans and contests provide opportunities for interactive communication. In addition to the vans and contests having stalls at local fairs, demonstrations and sampling are effective interactive communication methods, along with announcements and film shows.

As the quality of contact is important, companies send their marketing team along with their vans. Colgate–Palmolive has supply vans which offer free samples and screen video films on oral hygiene. 'Agri–Net' is a channel targeted at farmers operated by an agency called Lonestar. A team from Lonestar comprising a supervisor and two agricultural officials tour villages specified by the client company, and hold video presentations to educate farmers about certain products. Glaxo laboratories promoted its veterinarian medicinal herbs and Rallis India its pesticide range in this manner.

Contests involving consumers can be interactive and help create awareness, knowledge and trial too (see Box 7.5).

Box 7.5
Contests Involving the Consumer

GTC requests consumers to smoke four or five unidentified brands of cigarettes and spot the GTC brand. The blind tasting test helps the winners to easily recognise the GTC brand. Other typical contests involve building tower stacks with cigarette packets or locating buried treasure. The entry ticket is a cigarette packet and so the game provides a good method for inducing trial (Mukherjee, 1993).

Stalls at local fairs can also be made interactive. Brooke Bond adopts tea-stalls that tempt villagers to sample its products by offering free cups of tea. Geoffrey Manners participates in village *melas*, where it's salesmen who are dressed in white aprons to resemble doctors, extol the virtues of Anacin (Das Gupta and Menon, 1990). In addition to stalls, other points of contact are also utilised. Sunstar lubricants prints leaflets in regional languages, attends panchayat meetings and participates in agricultural meets to promote its products (Ghosh and Krishnaswamy, October 1997).

Demonstrations and Sampling: Marketers find it effective to give demonstrations of their products as these educate the buyer. Some demonstrations provide or allow a trial usage of the product, thus building brand awareness (see Box 7.6).

Box 7.6
Demonstration and Sampling to build Brand Preference

HLL advertises its detergents not through a catchy punch line on the ability to remove stains, but through tangible benefits—washing clothes for free. People hand over their dirty clothes on the spot, and wait in a queue to have them laundered. The method also helps HLL instruct rural consumers in the use of detergents, which is essential to convert them from laundry soaps.

When Asian Paints wanted to apply the sampling strategy on rural consumers thronging to the Pola fair in Maharashtra, it did not hand out trial tins of the paint. Instead it chose to home in on the ritual bullock-cart races. Before this race, owners usually bathe their champions and paint bright colours on their horns, reason, Asian Paints associates itself with the event. It handed out 100–200 gm. packets as opposed to its one and two kilogram tins, with its mascot 'Gattu' conspicuously printed on the packing (Mukherjee, 1993).

> Usha International, a manufacturer of sewing machines, sought to create excitement so that the brand is remembered and preferred. They ran sewing schools in villages that offered short-term tailoring courses for women.

The Emerging Non-conventional Media

Audio-visual Van: This is a vehicle that goes to selected villages and towns on weekly market days to communicate the benefits of the product in question in a way that is relevant to the target audience. Each van is festooned with a banner or painted in gay colours. It uses display boards whenever it stops to address the populace and its repertoire includes audio, video, film playback equipment, microphones and other demonstration facilities. It also passes out product literature and can conduct market surveys if required (see Box 7.7).

Box 7.7
Colgate–Palmolive's Promotion through Video Vans

Colgate–Palmolive is determined to draw more than half of its revenue from rural India by 2003, up from about 30 percent now. It spent five times more on rural marketing in 1996 than in 1991.

To get a foothold in the rural market, consumer product manufacturers cannot rely on conventional Madison Avenue marketing techniques. So marketers are turning to half-hour 'infomercials' broadcasted through the countryside in video vans.

Many Indians in rural areas have never handled products like shampoo and toothpaste. According to Colgate–Palmolive, fewer than 15 percent of rural Indians regularly use a dentifrice. For generations they have used charcoal powder and indigenous plants, such as the neem tree, to

---

cleanse their teeth. 'If they just saw the toothpaste tube, they wouldn't know what to do with it,' says Maitri Kumar, the company's marketing manager.

But they find out once the video van bumps into town. In Andarsul, a dusty village of 10,000 in the state of Maharashtra, a van decked out with oversize 'dummy' Colgate toothpaste tubes arrives on market day. It is the first time the van has called on Andarsul, which draws farmers and field workers from nearby hamlets to its weekly market.

Over the blare of a popular movie melody, a marketer invites shoppers to the van. He also throws open the rear door, revealing a video screen. Before long, about a 100 men and children have jostled for a viewing spot (women generally don't go to market in the Indian countryside).

In one scene of the 27-minute infomercial, villagers Kamla and Vijay are about to spend their wedding night together. As a passionate Vijay bends over to kiss his bride, she pulls away in disgust. He asks her what's wrong. She's embarrassed to say. The attentive audience is puzzled until it realizes the problem is Vijay's bad breath.

As the story unfolds through dialogue, song and dance, the newly weds consult a dentist and eventually reconcile. The message is clear: Colgate is good for your breath, teeth—and love life. After the dentist explains that traditional oral hygiene methods such as charcoal powder, are ineffective and even harmful, the video ends with Kamla, Vijay and their neighbours brushing their teeth.

The audience applauds enthusiastically and then rushes to get free samples at a stall beside the van. A Colgate marketer demonstrates how to use the toothpaste and a toothbrush. To encourage parents to buy a tube, he offers free Colgate brushes to a few children, only to leave many little hands grabbing for more.

A typical day for the audio-visual van operator includes identifying and arriving at the village *haat* in the morning, and establishing a suitable base. Where *haat* takes place on both sides of the road, the van is generally mobile throughout the day. Announcements are made through a public address system, and an audio capsule of about 20 minutes is played at least half a dozen times throughout the day.

Posters and handbills are distributed and product demonstrations and samplings are held. If the client or sponsor has provided stocks and a distributor's salesman is present, direct consumer sales are also made.

In the evenings, film shows or film-based programmes are held which inevitably draw huge crowds. This variety entertainment is interspersed by commercials and advertisement films of the client's products. Market research and retail surveys are also carried out during the day, if the client's brief so specifies.

Vans and video vans have had a mixed record. While some marketers have found them very useful to communicate and promote their products in rural markets, other marketers do not find the vans viable on a continuous basis. The weakness of this system can be attributed to the sheer logistics of such an exercise; complicated further by bad weather, road conditions, local body regulations, incorrect identification of villages, break downs and human fatigue (see Box 7.8).

Box 7.8
Audio-visual Promotion

The video van is an outgrowth of political campaigning. J. K. Jain, a New Delhi doctor, first used these vans in 1987 to spread propaganda for an opposition party that was denied air time on state-run television. Between elections, the vans were idle, so Dr. Jain approached consumer goods companies in 1989. Since then his fleet has grown from 28 to 125. Each van typically visits three villages a day.

Consumer companies generally deploy vans year round, except for three months during the monsoon season. Dr. Jain charges Rs. 88,000 ($2,520) a month for a van, which comes outfitted with video gear and a generator. (Colgate–Palmolive hires 85 vans at a time from a variety of companies.) In addition to the van rental, there is the cost of market research to identify promising villages and then to build a distribution system.

India's leading consumer products company, Hindustan Lever Ltd., estimates that the cost per contact of promoting a product in the countryside is four to five times higher than in the cities. But it reckons that the annual growth for personal care products and laundry detergent is about three times higher in the rural market as compared to the urban market.

Video van marketing should be seen in the context of the absence of an alternative, says Harish Manwani, director of personal products at HLL, which is a subsidiary of the Anglo-Dutch Unilever PLC. N. Jayaraman, marketing director at Bombay based Colgate–Palmolive India, is convinced that video vans have helped double toothpaste consumption in rural India since 1990. (According to the company, the annual rural consumption is 30 grams per person, compared with 160 grams per urban Indian and about 400 grams per person in the US.)

Not everyone is a believer. Britannia Industries Ltd., India's largest maker of biscuits and other snacks, discontinued video van marketing after three years. Raghu Chowdhury, who oversees sales operations, believes that it is too difficult to monitor. As he sees it, too many variables can undermine a van's impact, including where local authorities allow the vehicle to park, the level of dedication of the van's staff and weather conditions.

Point-of-Purchase (POP) Channels: This comprises a series of audio-visual sites located in shops in rural feeder towns. A typical installation consists of a colour television, a video cassette recorder (VCR) and a generator. Entertainment programmes are aired with advertisements (see Box 7.9).

Box 7.9
POP Channels

Lonestar Communications launched a fixed audio-visual network operating in markets that serviced rural buyers. In the second year, the network had 25 centres in Uttar Pradesh and 80 in Gujarat. Brands like Tulsi Mix, Pan Parag, Baba Zarda and Philips Bulbs were the initial users of the POP channel.

While the POP channel serves as a permanent network with audio-visual sites predetermined by Lonestar, clients also have the option of choosing their own locations depending on a brand's requirements. One such network is the 'Dhaba Network'. The idea of the Dhaba Network emanated at a time when Modi Rubber was keen to promote its RL-8 truck tyres. As the target audience was primarily the truck driver, the software was specifically programmed for them (Rajan, 1992).

Decision Implications

The marketer needs to use multiple media to communicate to the rural consumers who are geographically spread out. Marketers can efficiently reach rural consumers through popular television programmes. Advertising just before switching over to the national network provides good value for the media spend. A marketer can use the radio as an effective medium any time during the day but not late at night.

A marketer can effectively use different media for targeting strategy. It is useful to use mass media, including television for products targeted at upmarket rural consumers. Products targeted at the average income consumers in rural areas require interpersonal communication for persuasive promotion. This is to supplement mass media. Mailers can be used for product or brand launches to influence the literate who are an important segment of the opinion leaders. The mailers for consumer durables can be sent to those in service and farmers, while for farm inputs the tractor owners can be targeted.

A marketer can use different media to achieve different objectives. The press can be used for certain products. In situations where electronic media and press do not reach, outdoor media can be used. Advertisers can use wall paintings to effectively create awareness of brands or for brand reminders. This should be through the use of visuals. Media like puppetry or drama or putting a message on novel objects or on animals creates interest and grabs the attention of the rural consumer.

Marketers can use processions, tableaus and contests to build awareness and to communicate a product position. At many of the points of contacts like fairs, weekly markets or village wells or post offices, the use of audio-visual presentations, contests, dramatic presentations, setting up stalls can be educative and bring about attitude change. Demonstrations and sampling are highly effective tools for creating awareness, education and conviction among the rural audience. Promotion through retailers using opinion leaders and efforts to create satisfied customers are effective means to influence attitude of the rural consumers. The awareness, knowledge and attitude is also achieved through audio-visual vans and a network of fixed audio-visual sites.

References

Baptist, Vinod, 'Promotion by Channel Members in Rural Markets'. an unpublished report submitted as part of the PGDBM Course, XLRI, Jamshedpur, 1992.

Chandra, Prafulla, T.V., 'Communicating Health Information to Rural People', *Kurukshetra*, February, 1992.

Das Gupta, Surajeet and Menon, Ramesh, 'Rural Markets: The Call of Consumerism', *India Today*, July 15, 1990.

Das, Mukund and Sen, Somnath, 'Commercial Aspect: The Rural Way', *A&M*, October, 1991.

Das, Sandeep, 'Advertising in Rural Markets: Message Effectiveness', an unpublished report submitted as part of the PGDBM Course, XLRI, Jamshedpur, 1994.

Ghosh, Joydeep and Krishnaswamy, Chetan, 'The Rural Rush', *The Week*, Vol. 15, No. 44, 1997.

Mukherjee, Biman, 'The Fairground as Battlefield', *Business Today*, December 7–12, 1993.

Rajan, Ravi, 'Hooking on to a New Channel', *Brand Equity*, August 12, 1992.

Ray, Siddhartha, 'A Bird's Eye View', *A&M*, May 1–15, 1998.

Sarkar, Bashab, 'Other side of the Coin', *A&M*, May 1–15, 1998.

Shirali, Aresh, 'A Matter of Perceptions', *A&M*, February, 1993.

Sirbhaiya, Anupam, 'The Role of Mass Media and Interpersonal Communication as a Source of Information for the Rural Consumer', an unpublished report submitted as part of the PGDBM course, XLRI, Jamshedpur, 1994.

EIGHT

Retailer as a Route to the Rural Market

*This chapter looks at the critical issues in distributing through
the rural retail system. The retail system is important given
the predominance of this system in servicing the rural consumer. The influences on distribution are identified and
analysed to assist the marketing manager in distribution decisions. The influence of consumer behaviour, characteristics
of retailers and behaviour of the channel on distribution of
products are examined.*

Accessing Rural Markets

Accessing rural markets presents a challenge to the marketer
as these markets are geographically spread out with a large
number of retail outlets. The rural retail system is, therefore,
the predominant mechanism to reach and service the rural
consumers. This is achieved by a system of more than two
million village shops. The tasks before the marketer are:

- To ensure that the product reaches the rural retail outlet;
- To motivate the retailer in rural markets to stock a product
  or a brand. This is important given the limited number of
  items on the rural retail shelf. It is also critical as higher
  dealer generation results in higher reach among consumers
  and, therefore, a higher market share (see Table 8.1).

Table 8.1
Dealer Penetration and Market Share

	% Dealer	% Household	% Volume Share
TEA	65	79	-
Taaza	35	14	8
Tata	22	9	6
Lipton Tiger	17	6	2
3 Roses	13	6	3
SHAMPOO	55	38	-
Clinic	77	63	47
Lux	16	13	7
Chik	23	9	5
SKIN CREAM	37	18	-
Fair & Lovely	11	65	46
Pond's cold cream	14	11	13
Vicco Vani. Cream	12	3	3
SHAVING CREAM	37	9	-
VI-John	62	39	41
Palmolive	23	12	10
Godrej	12	10	6

Source: *ORG-MARG*, 2000

Though promotion and distribution are important, it is critical to motivate the channels to enable the products to be economically distributed. Marketers must address this issue by identifying influences on distribution and drawing inferences. The important influences on distribution to rural markets are:

• Purchase behaviour of consumers;
• Characteristics of retailers; and
• Behaviour of the channel.

Consumer Purchase Behaviour Implications for Distribution

There was a time when rural consumers purchased most of their requirements from nearby towns. Recently it has been observed that there has been a greater shift towards purchasing locally. This phenomenon has important implication for the rural marketer. There is a need to access retailers in towns and larger villages and promote products there. Products that are purchased locally must be available in the smaller retail outlets in villages. Gillette for instance, ensures that their product is well distributed all over the country; therefore they expect this effort to also result in thier products reaching rural areas through rural retailers (Ghosh and Krishnaswamy, 1997).

Consumer loyalty can be to the brand or to the retailer. It follows that the type of consumer loyalty has implications for a marketer. The influence of the retailer is perceived to be high in rural markets (Goyal, 1986), more so for durables (Velayudhan and Suri, 1996). In rural areas, loyalty to the shop rather than to the brand is higher, but not significantly so. It has been observed that the retailer influence is greater in rural markets, however, it is the knowledge of the brand that influences choice (Velayudhan, 1998).

The consumer loyalty pattern also suggests that promotion by the retailer is more important in rural markets. Literature suggests that promotion by the retailer supplements the efforts at creating brand knowledge in rural markets. A promotion of the benefits of the product or brand along with distribution effort is observed in the rural markets for instance in fast moving consumer goods (see Box 8.1).

Box 8.1
Promotion to Consumer and Servicing Retailers

- Colgate–Palmolive has supply vans that offer free samples and screens video films on oral hygiene. Vans are supplemented with bicycle vendors who go to those villages where the vans cannot access.
- Godrej has vans that play music and announce free gifts in the village square. The van then goes to a few shops in the villages to sell their product (Das Gupta and Menon, 1990).

The Rural Retail System: Characteristics of Retailers and their Influence on Distribution Strategies

Consumer loyalty to the retailer and the influence of the retailer on consumer choice suggests the need to examine the rural retail system. The characteristics of retailers and the retailer/channel behaviour are analysed to arrive at channel decisions (see Figure 8.1).

The retailer characteristics examined here are:

- Rural Market Spread;
- Retail Premises;
- Retail Shelf; and
- Stock Turnover.

Rural Market Spread: The rural market comprises small dispersed village settlements, infrequent retail outlets and low off-take per retailer. The high distribution cost due to the geographical spread and the low volumes result in a barrier to the entry of products in the rural market. The high distribution costs become a barrier when volumes are low. To build volumes there is a need to invest in distribution, but

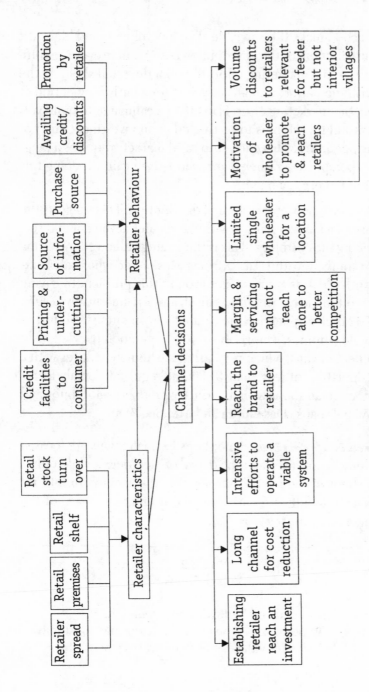

Figure 8.1 Retailer System and Channel Decisions

high costs make this unviable. The low volumes and high cost of distribution, or the 'distribution cost–volume cycle' require a substantial marketing effort to reach the retail shelf. As the distribution effort remains unviable for a fairly long period of time, the marketing effort is in effect a campaign to build volumes and therefore is to be treated as an investment and not an expenditure. This entry into rural markets requires a long-term perspective rather than a short-term gain. Keeping this in mind, there is a need:

- To have a low cost system of distribution. This suggests the use of a longer channel with the retailer at the tail end servicing the customer. This is the strategy followed by Nirma to compete with HLL. Nirma relies on the wholesaler network. HLL is trying to get around this problem by giving credit to the distributors (Ghosh and Krishnaswamy, 1997).
- To efficiently service the channels in an intensive effort to build volumes. The HLL strategy 'operation harvest', uses a fleet of vans, which regularly visits remote villages with a population of less than 5, 000 at regular intervals to re-stock small shops with its primary products—Lifebuoy and Wheel soaps (Das Gupta and Menon, 1990).

Retail Premises: The shops in small towns are located on rented premises and make use of electricity, while only a few shops in the feeder villages have this facility. In interior villages retailing is a part-time chore unlike the case of the retailer in town (see Box 8.2).

Box 8.2
Village Shops

In a study conducted by ICICI it was found that:
- Only 40 percent of shops in small towns had electricity while in feeder villages this figure was 11 percent.

- The shops in town were located on rented premises while in the interior villages in 88 percent of the cases the shops are on owned premises and without electricity.
- In feeder villages four fifths of the shops have one person working full time but in interior villages 70 percent have two or three persons working on a part time basis.
- Over two fifths of the retail outlets stocked eight to nine standard product categories.
- It was found that three fourth of the outlets which stocked eight to nine product categories kept four items or less in each category while one fourth had five to six items in each category.
- The total number of items stocked in retail outlets was about 50 in interior villages and 115 in feeder villages.
- The stock turnover ratio in the study is the number of times the stock is sold in a month. This is obtained by dividing the stock level to monthly off-take. This ratio for toiletries in interior villages was close to unity, while in the feeder villages two thirds had a ratio in the range of two to three. The ratio of one indicates that on an average, one month stock was available in interior village shops while shops in feeder villages maintained stocks for two or three months. The value of stock turnover ratio in the town had a wider spread and higher values in the range of three, or even over five, because of a wide variety of products stocked.

The maintenance costs for retail outlets in interior villages is low with most of the cost spent on travelling and transportation. This suggests that if the product or brand can be delivered to the outlet or if the travelling or transportation cost is compensated then the retailer in the interior village would prefer this product or brand.

Retail Shelf: It was also observed that most retail outlets stocked a few standard product categories while their counterparts in interior villages stocked fewer product categories.

These outlets also carried very few items within a category. The number of items per product category stocked was again lower in interior villages as compared to feeder villages or towns.

The scarcity of products available on the retail shelf in the interior villages suggests that the suppliers of these products need to deliver more products to these outlets. This is necessary if they want to have a significant presence in rural markets.

The study carried out by ICICI indicates that products like toiletries, cosmetics, certain packaged foodstuffs (biscuits, sweets, toffees and packaged vanaspati) packaged tea, bidis and to a lesser extent cigarettes, were widely stocked. Stationery items used by school children, matchboxes and kerosene lamps/ lanterns, were other popular items in interior villages.

Stock Turnover: The ICICI study indicates the average value of stocks per product category in the interior villages. The average value of stocks per product category in the interior villages is about a third of that in the feeder village. The average value of stocks of all packaged goods in interior villages was about a fourth of that in the feeder village. The monthly off - take for packaged products was only slightly more in feeder villages as was compared to interior villages. The variation is in the composition with a larger off-take of packaged foodstuffs and tobacco compared to other products in the interior villages; while in feeder villages toiletries had a higher off-take as compared to other product categories. Some of the retail outlets in the feeder villages had a higher turnover and served as semi-wholesalers. The stock turnover ratio (stock level to monthly off-take) for toiletries in interior villages was much less than that in feeder villages, less again than that observed for shops in town.

The low off-take, low stocks and lower stock turnover ratio reinforces the earlier observation that the number of products and items stocked is low in the interior villages. This effectively locks up the retail shelf space by the existing products and brands leaving no room for new products and brands. The marketer has to ensure that his product and brand is on the shelf as otherwise the competitors' brand will occupy the shelf instead. This would require a combination of margin, credit and servicing that is superior to that of the competitor. Delhi based Sun Star Lubricants is using a combination of low pricing and incentives to distributors to extend its reach to rural areas (Ghosh and Krishnaswamy, 1997).

Behaviour of the Channel

Understanding channel behaviour has a critical influence on channel decisions. The ability to influence the retailer to stock and promote products requires identifying the manner in which the retailer performs his business. Channel behaviour dimensions examined include:

- Credit Facilities to Customers;
- Pricing by the Channel;
- Reason for Stocking a Product/Brand;
- Information Source and Influence on the Retailer;
- Purchase Source for the Retailer;
- Channel Credit;
- Channel Promotion; and
- Promotion by the Retailer.

Credit Facilities to Customers: The extension of credit facilities by retailers to customers varies by location and by product. In a study by ICICI it was observed that the extension of credit facilities to consumers is practically non-existent in towns but in interior villages it is common. In another study, variations were also observed according to the products. Credit facility is given on essential commodities like rice, oil, etc., but not for packaged goods (Kilaru, 1994). There is a need for additional information before drawing firm conclusions on this aspect of retailer behaviour.

Pricing: Some retailers in interior villages charge more than the maximum retail price. They justify overcharging by pointing out that they spend time and money to fetch the products from wholesalers. This in turn suggests that higher margins are sought by channel members in rural markets. This inference is supported as it is observed that festival discounts given by the manufacturers to wholesalers or retailer normally contribute to increasing stock levels in the shops. These concessions are almost never passed on to consumers (Kilaru, 1994).

A rural wholesaler may deliberately undercut the price of a fast-moving brand in order to increase the traffic in his shop. When this happens to a brand then it is possible that others also cut their price of the brand resulting in a lower margin for the wholesalers leading to a lack of interest in the brand. To overcome this, a marketer may only use a single or a few wholesalers to sell to retailers. This would avoid undercutting and sustain interest in the brand. The strategy of using limited dealers was followed by the marketer of a leading brand of luggage products. They followed this strategy for their low-priced suitcases targeted at the rural markets. They have exclusive dealers in a market dominated by small players selling unbranded moulded luggage. Exclusive dealers are motivated to push the branded suitcases to quality and brand-conscious rural buyers, anticipating an attractive return as compared to the unbranded item (see Box 8.3).

Box 8.3

Limiting the Number of Dealers to Prevent Undercutting

The moulded luggage industry has a number of small players. A leading brand faced a formidable problem in one of its rural markets as this market was dominated by the smaller brands that competed on price. The dealers purchased from suppliers and sold the brand at a discount. Therefore margins were low for all the members in the channel. The brand had an image in this market. In the rural markets, support from dealers would not be forthcoming for a high priced product selling low volumes and carrying low margins because of price competition. The marketer of the branded product restricted its dealership and this allowed holding the price and therefore yielding better margins for the dealer. The result was an increase in the motivation of these dealers to push the brand in this market.

Reason for Stocking a Product or Brand: Rural retailers stock a particular item usually because consumers request it and to a lesser extent because of the wholesaler's push or because a competitor stocks the item (Kilaru, 1994).

This implies that the marketer has to direct his effort to promoting the brand both to the consumer and to the wholesaler. This supports the inference based on the observation of loyalty of the rural consumer to both the brand and the retailer. Motivating dealers to promote the brand requires restricting their number. Limiting the number of dealers prevents undercutting and improves their margin.

Information Source and Influence: A study covering 25 retailers in seven villages of Deoria district of Uttar Pradesh brought out the importance of the wholesaler. According to the study, the wholesaler is the most important source of information for the retailer. The wholesaler is also the most important influence on the retailer (Kilaru, 1994).

This means that the marketer would do well to motivate the wholesaler to get the retailer in the rural market to stock its products, more so for newer products. This is the approach followed by Nirma (Ghosh and Krishnaswamy, 1997).

Purchase Source: A study of retailers in Uttar Pradesh indicated that retailers in interior areas are not visited by agents of distributors, therefore they go to town or feeder village once or twice a month to buy their stock. Retailers in feeder villages purchase items like cosmetics, toiletries, detergents, and packaged foodstuffs from agents of distributors who visit their shop at regular intervals and deliver these items (Kilaru, 1994).

Implication is that it is necessary for marketers of cosmetics, toiletries, detergents and packaged foodstuffs to ensure that the products are delivered at the feeder villages. These are the items that are also stocked in the shops in interior villages and therefore effective promotion to retailers/wholesalers in the feeder village is necessary for pushing these items to retail outlets in the interior villages.

Channel Credit: Small retailers and retailers in interior villages make their purchases in cash while larger retailers in feeder markets buy on credit (Kilaru, 1994).

The marketer has to ensure that the channel not only services the product requirements but also extends credit to the retailers in feeder villages.

Channel Promotion: Retailers in interior villages do not avail of discount schemes as they prefer not to stock more, while this may not be so for retailers in the feeder markets (Kilaru, 1994).

Discount schemes should be targeted to retailers in feeder market and are usually ineffective in interior markets. Discounts for retailers in feeder markets are relevant as the additional stocks carried by outlets in the feeder markets meet the needs of not only the consumer but also the retailer in the interior villages.

Promotion by the Retailer: When retailers in rural markets promote products to the consumers, the rural consumer expects the retailer to provide information and suggestions about the product. This is partly supported by studies on consumer behaviour. Retailers are influenced by the commission and credit received by them in their recommendation of brands (Kilaru, 1994).

Implication is that marketer is to provide attractive commission and credit facility to motivate the retailer to promote the brand.

Retailer–Consumer Reinforcing Behaviour

Consumer loyalty to the retailer is indicated to be higher in rural markets than in urban markets. Research studies quoted in this chapter indicate that the retailer stocks brands that the rural consumer buys and is reluctant to stock new items. This behaviour creates yet another barrier to the marketer of a new brand. Marketers need to consider alternative ways to reach the rural consumer instead of being totally dependent on the rural retail shops. This is required to break through the hurdles created by high cost and low volumes of the marketer, limited shelf space with retailers and limited opportunities for consumer to try out new brands. *Haats* and *melas* are options that are examined in the following chapter to break out of these barriers.

Decision Implications

The marketer can reach the rural consumers by effectively utilizing the rural retail system. Attractive margins and superior servicing should be used to persuade the rural retailer. The margins should compensate the rural retailers efforts to transport and stock products for long periods. Wholesalers are to be given support to increase volumes. Using a limited number of wholesalers is the key to hold their loyalty. The marketers may use a combination of attractive margins, credit and discount schemes to motivate larger outlets or wholesalers in feeder markets.

The marketer can build the rural distribution system using the van operations. The costs of van operations are to be allocated between distribution and promotion. The van used to supply to retailers is used also for promotion to consumers through either audio-visuals, demonstrations or sampling. The distribution costs in the initial year would be high because of low volumes and so this cost is to be treated as an investment and not expenditure. This is all the more true for products like cosmetics, toiletries and packaged goods. For marketers of new products (not brands), higher priced consumer goods, or goods for which the rural consumers would like to have variety, reaching the smaller towns may suffice for effective coverage of rural markets.

References

Das Gupta, Surajeet and Menon, Ramesh, 'Rural Markets : The Call of Consumerism', *India Today*, July 15, 1990.

Ghosh, Joydeep and Krishnaswamy, Chetan, 'The Rural Rush', *The Week*, Vol. 15, No. 44, 1997.

Goyal, 'Buyer Behaviour of Tractor Owners', *Indian Journal of Marketing*, Vol. 16, No. 10, 1986.

ICICI, 'Rural Marketing: A Pilot Study', Mumbai, 1979.

Kilaru, Sudheer, 'Study of Retailer Behaviour in Rural Market', An unpublished report prepared as part of PGDBM at XLRI, Jamshedpur, 1994.

Mukherjee, Biman, 'The Fairground as Battlefield', *Business Today*, December 7–21, 1993.

ORG-MARG, 'Marketing Gramifications : Mapping Rural Consumer Behaviour', 2000.

Velayudhan, Sanal Kumar, 'Buyer Behaviour in Rural Markets : A Study of Soap Market', *Productivity*, Vol. 39, No. 2, July–September, 1998.

Velayudhan, Sanal Kumar and Suri, B., 'Rural Market Response—A Tentative Study', *Management and Labour Studies*, Vol. 21, No. 1, 1996.

NINE

Haats and *Melas*

This chapter identifies the presence of a remarkable distribution system that is available to the rural marketer. The rural consumer looks forward to markets and fairs that are held on a regular basis in villages. These haats *and* melas *provide the marketer with a unique opportunity to access the rural consumer. Their characteristics and relevance to marketers is examined. An attempt is also made to understand their administration, the nature of transactions, type of traders, the location of stalls, coverage and prices of products that are available.*

Channel Variants in Rural Markets

The last chapter focused on the behaviour of the rural retailer and the issue of motivating distribution channels. However, distribution to rural markets is different from urban markets for multiple reasons. One of the main reasons is that the cost of reaching the outlets is higher for rural markets because of the geographical spread. There is also a difference due to the type of channels available to the marketer. A distinct feature of the rural markets is the presence of *haats* and rural fairs (see Box 9.1).

Box 9.1
Channel Variants in Rural Markets

One major characteristic that is not present in urban markets are *melas* and *haats* that play a significant role in the selling of goods and services.

- The importance of the country's 5,000 fairs are being recognised by marketers as the attendance at these fairs is believed to be over 100 million (Mukherjee, 1993).
- *Haats* are weekly markets. These markets reach a large number of potential rural consumers. A study suggests that six percent of all villages had permanent *haats* and another nine percent had temporary *haats* (Social and Research Institute, 1990).

Haats

These periodic markets are an important part of the rural way of life. The aspects that are examined here include:

- *Haats* as critical distribution channels in rural markets;
- Characteristics of *haats:*
  - an understanding
  - products and transactions
  - administration
- Trading and traders in *haats:*
  - traders and their products
  - trading location by specialization
  - trading system
  - market coverage by traders
  - measures used and trade margins

Haats as Critical Distribution Channels in Rural Markets

A study on *haats* indicated that despite the same products being available in the village shop, 58 percent of the visitors preferred to buy these from a *haat* because of better price, quality and variety. IMRB's rural market probe found that more than 25 percent of the 3,10,000 villages having a population below 500 do not have any shop and another 56 percent have between one to four small *pan/bidi* (corner shop kiosks) and/or provision shops selling limited quantities of soap, toothpaste, tea, etc. The availability of shops is a little better in the next category of villages with a population between 501 to 2000, totaling 2,50,000 but the sale is still not good enough in terms of cost-benefit equation for companies to reach the retailers. (Kashyap, 1998). *Haats* provide a very useful mechanism of reaching the interior rural markets. It is estimated that there are 47,000 *haats* held periodically in rural India (Kashyap, Pradeep 1998).

The importance of *haats* is greater in the interior, less prosperous villages. In the more fertile tracts, permanently located shops are more important as outlets of goods. Marketers use the *haats* and the permanent shops to effectively reach the rural consumers.

Characteristics of *Haats*

An Understanding: *Haats* are periodic markets. Periodic markets means that people assemble at a particular place at least once a week in order to buy and sell products. *Haats* operate in a weekly cycle. They may vary in the intensity of their transactions depending upon the season but they seem to have a fairly stable periodicity. They serve the village in which it is located and also the surrounding villages (Wanamali, 1981, p. 31). Each *haat* caters to the needs of a minimum of 10 to a maximum of 50 villages from where an average of 4,000 persons come to buy a range of daily necessities and services (Kashyap, 1998).

Consumers and traders who form a major part of the population attending these markets do not necessarily attach much importance to the population of the village in which the market is held. In their view, the importance of a market is based on the number of stalls it has, especially the number of stalls selling urban consumer goods (Wanamali, 1981). Most *haats* have an average of 314 stalls and a sale exceeding two million rupees per *haat* day. (Kashyap, 1998).

Large *haats* are held in bigger villages because of better road and transport connections and a higher purchasing power available in the host villages—4,300 are held in the 5,000+ category and another 10,300 in the 2,000 to 4,999 population villages (Kashyap, 1998).

Products and Transactions

The nature of transactions that interest the marketer are:

- The products that are bought and sold in these markets;
- Variation in the market activity in the day time and variation in the activity depending on the weekday.

In many periodic markets, agricultural and forest products and various village handicrafts are predominant goods. Urban consumer goods are also sold. These are sold from temporary stalls by travelling traders (Wanamali, 1981, p. 17).

There are identifiable variations, both during the day and the week, in the market activity of a periodic market. For example, during the day, produce is sold during the first half of any market meeting, whereas in the second half, urban consumer goods are purchased and leisure activities like drinking rice beer are more important.

During the week, on days other than the traditional market day, there is little trading activity in any market, except those holding *gudhdhi haats*, and those located in the urban centres (Wanamali, 1981, p. 43).

A *gudhdhi haat* has entertainment value where people gather essentially to watch cock-fights and drink rice beer. Here vegetable sellers and one or two snack food sellers are also seen doing brisk business. These vendors always belong to the villages holding the *gudhdhi haat* (Wanamali, 1981).

Administration: The government auctions the *haats*, and the contractor who wins the auction, administers them. The contractor collects taxes from the different types of traders, and allots stalls and areas for trading.

Newcomers are normally given a space which is normally not in a prime location. Sometimes, in order to discourage a newcomer, available space may be rented by the existing traders. In this manner by paying a nominal tax for a stall or two, traders appear to avoid real competition (Wanamali, 1981, p. 60).

Trading and Traders in *Haats*

Traders and their Products: The two major types of traders that have been observed in the periodic markets are the part-time and full-time traders. The part-time traders can be further sub-divided into two classes: the producer–sellers and the collector–sellers. The full-time traders can be categorised further into three classes: the selling–traders, the buying–traders and those engaged in services (see Figure 9.1).

- The producer–sellers deal in the following products: earthenware, bamboo ware, brooms, *dathuan*, ropes, vegetables, fruits, *moori* (puffed rice), paddy, rice, pulses, chicken, eggs, dry fish, fresh fish, meat, ducks and cattle.
- The collector–sellers deal in leaves, firewood, grass for fodder, *gunja, tisi, lac, mahua, tassar*, berries of various types and tamarind.
- The selling–traders deal in aluminium ware, brassware, cloth, ready-made garments, footwear, cosmetics, toiletries, stationery, plastic and rubber goods, biscuits, chocolates, provisions, kerosene, tobacco products, etc.
- The buying–traders deal in fruits, vegetables, chicken, *lac, mahua, gunja, tisi* and *tassar*.
- Those engaged in services include cycle mechanics, barbers, blacksmiths, carpenters, rice beer sellers, eatables, tea and coffee (Wanamali, 1981, p. 46).

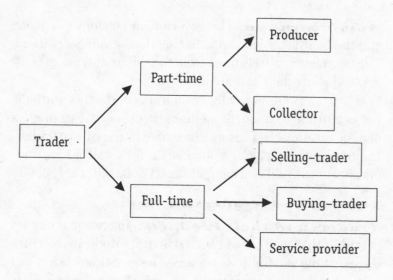

Figure 9.1 Type of Traders in Periodic Markets

Trading location: The location of stalls in a periodic market follow a pattern which is functionally organised. The location of the trader is based on the following factors:

- Specialization by goods;
- Perishability of goods;
- Goods that are likely to break.

The various traders are allotted space in such a manner that 'a specialist area', or traders trading in a particular type of good, converge in one area. The buying–traders specialising in the purchase of fruits and vegetables tend to locate themselves on the periphery of the market and along the tarmac road so that they can tap the producer–sellers efficiently and when their transactions are completed, depart from the market as quickly as possible. Vendors selling earthenware also locate themselves away from the main market centre in order to avoid the breakage of their goods in the bustle of the market. The distinguishing feature of this area is that it does not have any built up stalls of mud and bamboo, which are provided for the selling–traders, the buying–traders and those providing services.

Trading System: Almost all selling–traders obtain their goods from wholesale merchants in large markets in towns. This system is known as the *kalam* system, which involves the selling–traders obtaining the goods of a given value for a given period of time. At the end of that period, which is usually a week or a fortnight, the selling–traders are expected to return the total value of goods obtained initially to the wholesale merchants. This can be done in cash or in cash and kind (Wanamali, 1981, p.135).

A useful approach to tap the *haats* is to identify the traders who supply goods on credit to the small traders in the *haats*. These traders are located in the larger villages or small towns that feed the interior villages. The feeder market merchants referred to in this book are those traders who supply goods to the small traders visiting the *haats* surrounding the feeder market.

Market Coverage by Traders: The coverage of the *haats* by the trader depends upon:

- Products handled by the trader;
- The number of villages serviced by the *haat;*
- Distance of the *haat* from the trader's location;
- Nature of competition in the *haat;*
- Economic strength of the trader to compete;

Selling–traders dealing in goods which are used more frequently such as soaps, general provisions and fancy goods, travel up to six markets a week. Those selling goods which are used less frequently such as aluminium utensils, footwear, clothes and readymade garments, visit three and six markets a week (Wanamali, 1981, p. 136).

This is a tendency amongst the selling–traders to visit nodal markets where less important markets are located. This ensures that these are also served as most rural consumers from remote areas attend the larger and more important markets (Wanamali, 1981, p.146).

The smaller selling–traders appear to take advantage of the space-time sequence of *haats* in a number of ways. It seems to facilitate their movement from one market to another during the week without any economic or spatial conflict—where there are two market meetings on the same day, the nearest of the two is favoured. There are also some traders who visit distant markets in order to avoid competition from the more successful selling–traders who offer the same product and also from permanently located shops in the larger locations (Wanamali, 1981, p. 146).

The bigger selling–traders maximise their returns in a different manner. They give their goods on loan to small selling–traders (the *kalam* system) in addition to selling these goods themselves. Goods are loaned either for the day or for a week. This seems to be a more accepted and prevalent practice amongst big traders dealing in soaps, fancy goods, general provisions, clothes and ready-made garments. In almost all cases, the bases of such operations are those markets which are the nodes in a system. This locational characteristic of a market facilitates the maximisation of profits in two ways. In the first instance, big traders are able both to sell to consumers and to loan goods to small selling–traders. The small trader may operate in the same market as a big trader under the *kalam* system. Even here it results in the big trader spatially covering more of a system of markets than he would do on his own (Wanamali, 1981, p. 147).

Measures used and Trade Margins: A proper inquiry into prices of various goods sold by the producer–seller is almost impossible. An important reason is the absence of standardisation of weights and measures. Local measures made of the wood of the *karanj* tree, and leaf containers of various types act as standard measures along with the more modern metric weights.

Barter as a form of exchange is also prevalent in some markets. It is not uncommon to exchange a leaf full of salt with a leaf full of tobacco, the leaf sizes in question being different to accommodate the difference in the intrinsic values of the two commodities (Wanamali, 1981, p. 98).

The selling–traders have a mark-up on the wholesale price. The big trader charges five percent less than the percentages given (see Table 9.1) (Wanamali, 1981, p. 107).

Table 9.1
Mark-up on Wholesale Prices by Traders

Commodities	Mark-up in percentage
Cloth and ready-made garments	20 to 25
Footwear	15 to 20
Aluminium utensils	20 to 25
General provisions	15 to 20

Melas

Melas are a part of Indian culture. These are fairs where people converge for occasions, festivals or to commemorate other important events. By conservative estimates, at least 20,000 *melas* are held every year all over the country (Gosh, 1994).

Melas are very important to the marketer for the following reasons:

- They are invariably connected to religious festivals, which makes it obligatory for people to attend a *mela*.
- They are part of India's rural culture and history. Rural folk are always aware when and where the *mela* takes place.

- They take place around the time farmers sell their crops, which means that the rural consumer has surplus money to spend in the *melas*.
- They are usually joyous, lively affairs and create a holiday atmosphere. This atmosphere puts the consumers in a spending mood (Gosh, 1994).
- Farmers bring their families along. Women, who ordinarily are restricted from moving out of the village, have universal social sanction to visit the *mela*. Marketers can take advantage of this tradition to establish a face-to-face communication with women, which they would otherwise find difficult to accomplish as women seldom visit local markets (Kashyap, 1998).

Mela Mood: As described above, fairs held in rural markets are associated with festivals and are generally held after the harvest season. This is the time for the villagers to celebrate, as they are in a festive mood—willing to spend money and try new products. Variations, novelty, change and trials are part of the mood, which make this time ideal for marketers to launch new products in rural markets.

***Characteristics of* Melas:** The average number of stalls per *mela* is 854, the average sale per *mela* day ranges from a low of Rs 60,000 in Assam to Rs 8.8 million in Haryana. The duration of a *mela* varies from one to 45 days. A study indicated the average number of visitors as 0.76 million per *mela* (the reason for this high figure is because some of the biggest *melas* such as Kumbh, Pushkar and Sonepur were included in the study).

Unlike the *haats*, which cater primarily to the essential needs of the local people, *melas* cater to a much larger population, both rural and urban, with more sophisticated factory-made products. Almost half the outlets in the *melas* sell manufactured goods (Kashyap, 1998).

Decision Implications

Marketers need to supplement their sales through the retail channel through *haats*. *Haats* reach rural consumers efficiently, as each *haat* serves a number of villages. *Haats* can be used to sell products that are regularly used including packaged foods, toiletries, cosmetics and certain low-value durables like utensils.

Haats offer an opportunity for sales promotion campaigns and also for new product launches. Demonstrations are essential to convert customers at *haats* since the attitude of rural buyers is utilitarian. *Haats* can be used for sampling of new products or increased penetration of existing products. Stalls can be set up later in the morning if the marketer plans to carry out product promotions in the *haats*.

Marketers can effectively reach a number of *haats* by servicing a limited number of selling traders who cover multiple *haats*. However, the focus must be on the large-selling traders for coverage and this is to be supplemented with a few small-selling traders. The latter is to ensure effective coverage of distant markets. The selling traders can be effectively tapped by identifying wholesale merchants in feeder markets who service these traders and offer them incentives.

A marketer can use *melas* to create awareness and preference for products and brands as they provide an excellent opportunity for promotion. A large population can be accessed at a fraction of the cost as compared with television, video vans or other equally expensive media options. Marketers keen to target women can use *melas* to establish face-to-face communication. Here, a suitable approach for promotion is to use a religious theme. This can be used to bring out the advantages of the product or even to get the attention and interest of the rural consumer. This is appropriate as *melas* are usually associated with religious festivals.

A marketer can use *melas* to introduce new products and brands for durable or non-durable products. As a festive mood prevails, novelty and change are welcome. Sellers of durable goods can use *melas* to improve sales and brand promotion. This is because *melas* are held immediately after the harvest season and the rural consumers have more money at this time.

References

Gosh, Aparisim, 'The New Rules of Rural Marketing', *Business World*, April, 1994.

Kashyap, Pradeep, 'Selling to the Sons of the Soil', *Strategic Marketing*, August–October, 1998.

Mukherjee, Biman, 'The Fairground as Battlefield', *Business Today*, December 7–21.

Social and Research Institute, 'Villages of India', A study of the Indian Market Research Bureau, 1990.

Wanamali, Sudhir, 'Periodic Markets and Rural Development in India', B.R. Publishing Corporation, New Delhi, 1981.

TEN

A Competitive Strategy for Rural Markets

The earlier chapters have examined each of the strategy elements based on market characteristics, consumer and channel behaviour. Strategy is influenced to a large extent by the competitive situation. This perspective is used to organise the approach to strategy for rural markets. Competition originates from existing players, new players and substitutes. Market development is an option selected by existing players in response to the entry of smaller competitors. New entrants look at ways to create shelf space for the product, or establish a symbiotic relationship with existing players. The response to such entry strategies is examined. The peculiarities of rural markets require a focus not only on size and market share of the players, but also on the competition from the unorganised sector, duplicates and imitation. Competing with substitutes is also analysed. A critical aspect that affects implementation of strategy in such a vast market is also examined.

Competition in Rural Markets

Competition in rural markets is varied in nature (see Figure. 10.1), and a marketer faces competition not only from other brands but also from substitutes, especially in places where

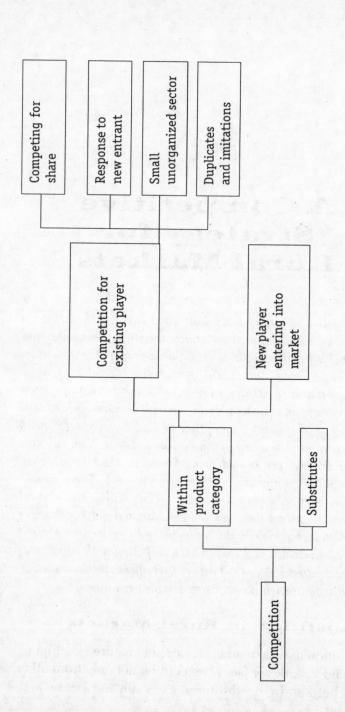

Figure 10.1 Competitive Scenario

the product is new to the consumer. Such situations are quite common in rural markets. Competition for existing brands can be from other brands, from new players, small unorganised sectors, duplicates and imitations. The task for a new player entering the market is difficult given the advantages that entrenched brands have in rural markets. Options and approaches under each of the above situations are examined.

Entry Strategy for a New Player

The entry of a new brand in the rural market is a difficult proposition. This is because in rural markets the pioneer creates a lasting impression and loyalty to such brands is higher. In the case of an organisation entering the rural markets for the first time, the sheer size of the market in geographic terms poses a formidable challenge in accessing retailers. Entry strategies in such situations include:

- Efforts to create shelf space for the product; and
- To establish a symbiotic relationship with an existing marketer.

Efforts to Create Shelf Space for the Product: Consumer pull creates a space for the brand on the retail shelf that is difficult to replace. In such a situation competitive efforts that rely on positioning alone are unlikely to create a sufficient impact. A brand that tries to break the loyalty of the rural consumer needs to not only make an extra effort in creating a position for itself in the consumer's mind but also have distribution muscle to create shelf space in the village shop (see Box 10.1).

Box 10.1
Creating Space in the Village Shop

- A study on the response of consumers to marketing efforts in villages around Jamshedpur was carried out. The Nirma vs Wheel drama was also enacted in these markets. Nirma created a position amongst the rural consumers with its media efforts as an 'effective cleaning product'. The Wheel launch followed also with media support but was not perceived to be as effective in cleaning. Nirma was available from its distributor located in Jamshedpur unlike Wheel which pushed its brand into the interior markets. Consumer preference for Nirma was not supported with consistency in availability. The consumer switch to Wheel helped gain its share of the market (Velayudhan and Suri, 1996).

- 'Hariyali Safar' is a project of Henkel SPIC India to penetrate the rural market. Under the project, the company has divided the country into a 100 blocks with one super stockist for each block. Each super stockist is reached through vans. The super stockist is expected to service 15 to 20 dealers in semi-urban areas. By the end of 2001, Henkel expects to have a 100 super stockists reaching 1500 to 2000 dealers. It is also introducing economy packs and sachets: Henko compact sachets, 50 gm. Margo soaps, 20 gm. Fa talcs and 250 gm. Mr. White detergent packs. It expects its current media campaign to generate acceptance of its brand in the rural market (Iyer, 2000).

A Symbiotic Relationship with an Existing Player: Size and relative capability also has an influence on strategy. One of the strategies common to large organisations that have technology and resources but no access into interior markets, is establishing a symbiotic relationship with organisations that have had a previous presence in rural markets.

Reach-Resources Symbiotic Relationship:
These are tie-ups between large organisations that do not have a distribution network and organisations that have geographical reach. The large organisation with technology or resources gets the access required for its products and the partnering firm is benefited as this synergetic relationship reduces the costs of distribution and therefore increases its profitability (see Box 10.2).

Box 10.2
Symbiosis as an Entry Strategy

Mulkanoor Primary Agricultural Cooperative Society (MPACS) is located in Mulkanoor, a village in the Karimnagar District of Andhra Pradesh. In the late seventies this society entered into an agreement with Pioneer Seeds for hybrid maize seeds. Pioneer seeds would provide the foundation seeds for producing the second stage foundation seeds. The society then produced the second stage foundation seeds and marketed them in bags with the name 'Pioneer' on one side and 'MPACS' on the other. The area of operation was the entire district. The seeds received immediate acceptance because of the farmer's loyalty in the local society and because of its ability to reach all the dealers with whom they had established relationships. The relationship helped both the partners to utilise their capabilities profitably.

This strategy is useful for products, particularly durables, that require frequent servicing (see Box 10.3).

Box 10.3
'Exide Industries Ltd. to Woo Unorganised Sector'

Exide Industries Ltd. has developed a strategy targeted at owners of tractors and heavy commercial vehicles in the farm sector code-named 'Kisan Project', through which it hopes to increase turnover of the company by Rs 600 million in 2000–2001. The tractor and HCV segment demands 3 million batteries, which constitute 30 percent of total demand in the country. Under the Rs 40 million crore rural marketing strategy, company officials will tour remote villages in Punjab and Haryana and will attempt to convert manufacturers of battery products in the unorganised sector into Exide dealers (*Business Standard*, May 26, 2000, p. 71).

Competition for Existing Players

Competition for existing brands in rural markets can be from a number of sources. These include:

- Competing for a share with existing players;
- Competition from a new entrant;
- Competing with small or unorganised players; and
- Competing against duplicates and imitations.

Competing for a Share with Existing Players: This situation is less likely in rural markets with competition mostly from the unorganised sectors and new players. The size and market share of the players influences strategy. The leader's strategy in the rural market is to expand the market. HLL consistently follows this strategy. They have launched a campaign to increase their presence in rural markets through their 'Operation Bharat' (see Box 10.4).

Box 10.4
Market Development Strategy of HLL and Rasna Enterprises

- In 1999, the soaps, detergents and personal product segments of HLL owed their growth strategy to a strong rural thrust. HLL launched its 'Operation Bharat', a 20 million household national sampling exercise for its personal products portfolio. As part of the campaign, low-priced sample packets of toothpastes, fairness creams, shampoos (Clinic Plus) and talcum powder (Ponds) were handed out to 20 million households.

  According to Dalip Sehgal, Head of Marketing (Personal Products) in HLL, 'the size of the pie will increase from the rural segment, not the urban segment. So the focus should be more on market development rather than market share at the moment'. (Zaheer, 1999)

- Rasna Enterprises is increasing its efforts in the rural markets in order to push sales of its main product, Rasna soft drink concentrate. Says Rasna Enterprise President, Raj Pinjani, 'Earlier, we relied totally on our wholesalers to push the product in the rural areas. Now we are going there ourselves, in order to get a feel of the market and promote the product directly'.

  In order to promote trials in the semi-urban and rural markets, Rasna launched its soft drink concentrate in sachets during the early nineties. The sachet was promoted using characters from the *Mahabharat* television serial. This year, Rasna has replaced these advertisements with the comedian Johnny Lever. The company is focusing on nine districts in the states of Maharashtra, Gujarat, Rajasthan, Uttar Pradesh and Tamil Nadu. A sales force regularly calls on retailers in these districts. Says Mr. Pinjani, 'It's remarkable the amount of goodwill a visit to the rural distribution network can generate. It builds enormous brand loyalty among the retailers, who in turn, push sales to the consumer' (Ganguly, 2001).

The fight for market share is an effort at positioning. In rural markets positioning is achieved through methods and media that compel the attention of the audience. Games and demonstrations are common. Eicher organizes tug-of-war contests between its own tractors and those of rival companies at the Pushkar fair. As the audience cheers, the Eicher tractor wins the contest, creating an emotive position for itself (Mukherjee, 1993).

Response to Competition from a New Entrant: When brands in the rural market are faced with new entrants, the best way to defend them is to strengthen the existing distribution system. Their access, servicing and delivery can be improved thereby preventing entry of other brands. With the increasing competition by different brands to Lifebuoy, the response has been to strengthen its distribution in the rural markets. This was supported by introducing other brands too. The 'Charminar' cigarettes are delivered by a combination of vans and bicycles to the trader in the interiors. Any weakness in distribution is an opportunity for a new entrant which can have disastrous consequences for the existing brand (see Box 10.5).

Box 10.5
Uttam *Beedis*

In the beginning of the eighties, Uttam *beedis* begain with family members rolling *beedis*, packing and selling these in and around Bhadrachalam, a small town in Andhra Pradesh. The leading brand in Bhadrachalam was PVS *beedis*. PVS *beedis* and Uttam *beedis* were both of average size. The retailers usually stocked PVS *beedis* as this was the fast moving brand. In 1983, for some reason there was a low stock of PVS beedis in shops. Uttam *beedis* seized this opportunity and ensured that their brand was available in the shops. Uttam *beedis* today has the leadership position in this market. In the nearby Kothagudam market, Uttam *beedis* has been trying for years now to make an entry but has failed to make a dent as retailers are unwilling to stock any other brands in that market other than the fast moving brands—PVS *beedis* and S *beedis*.

An effective recipe for defence of brands in rural markets is to provide the consumers with quality products that meet their needs by ensuring availability through systems that regularly service the channels. The loyalty of customers limits brand switching thereby ensuring that the retailers stock mostly this brand. The rural retailer does not maintain variety, as his ability to stock is low, therefore it is profitable to the retailer to stock only the fast-moving items and brands. It is when the popular brand is not available that the retailer looks for a new brand, forcing trial and a possible brand switch. A continuation of low or zero stock results in customers and retailers shifting loyalty to a new entrant.

Competing with Small or Unorganised Players: Large players face competition from smaller players on price and margins. They also find it difficult to match the lower price and attractive terms of the low-cost player. Even HLL has recently phased out Lipton Tea. This is a two-year-old, low-priced brand for rural markets, which had one of the highest recall values in the branded tea industry. The brand was withdrawn following competition from loose tea. The company has found that in many product categories, local and regional brands and poor infrastructure to reach the rural markets has affected volume growth. Companies like Hindustan Levers, and Marico are developing products with low prices and in sachets and pouches to meet competition from local players (Kala Vijayaraghavan and Anamika Rath, 2000). The strategic responses evidenced in such situations are:

- Strengthen existing access: media and channel;
- Offer a value for money proposition;
- Retention of dealer margins.

Strengthen Existing Access Media and Channel: Some marketers do not tamper with the product, packaging or its message. Their effort is to increase access/delivery. The decision areas of distribution and media are given more attention. Distribution is strengthened through van support and for promotion non-conventional media is preferred. (see Box 10.6).

Box 10.6
Typical Strategy in Rural Markets: Crane *Supari*

Crane betel nut powder is a leading brand of betel nut powder in South India. It is known for its quality and has a very strong consumer loyalty. The packs are sold in convenient price slots of 50 paise, Re 1, Rs 2 and Rs 5. The pack sizes include, apart from very small packs, packs of 25 gm., 50 gm., 100 gm., 250 gm. and half kg. There are six varieties of arecanut and brand building is through maintaining the taste. The product range includes both spicy and sweet supari.

The channel includes distributors, sub-distributors, wholesalers and retailers. The distributors are reached through company vehicles within three days of the receipt of requisition along with a draft for advance payment. In the case of rural markets, the distribution is once a month through trucks that follow an itinerary. In the case of smaller and interior areas, transporters are used. In addition to this, the company provides van support to distributors for delivering to rural markets. The company makes available to the rural distributors small vans with the condition that they carry only the Crane brand. The day's expenditure for the van is borne by the distributor who uses it.

The media used in rural markets include cable television, stickers and danglers, painting the sides of buses, wall paintings and shop paintings. Mimicry and dance drama were used in the early nineties, but no longer. Vans were used to create awareness and to provide brand knowledge in between songs that attracted attention. The vans were also painted with the brand message. This kind of promotion is no longer used as the company does not find them effective. A large part of the promotion to rural areas today is through stalls in fairs followed by wall paintings. Other media are used but to a limited extent.

The brand has a good image in the rural market but the presence of a large number of local and small brands competing on price restrict the market share. The rural market is large but because of price competition its major share is from the urban market. It is the leader in South India but its leadership is because of the urban market.

Offer a Value for Money Proposition: The second strategic response of the organised sector to competition from the unorganised sector is more aggressive. The effort to research and understand the market helps decide on distribution, media and repositioning effort.

The large brands usually compete on the value for money concept, introducing brands priced lower than the prices of their existing brands and in small package sizes having a lower unit price. The quality of the brand is promoted with the objective of appealing to the rural consumer who looks for quality products. Distribution efforts are intensified to provide better delivery and avoid stock problems. The repositioning effort is an important aspect of the strategy and the effect is much more dramatic than the increased access strategy. Experience of a leading brand of an optical whitener (a blue powder) in this respect provides an interesting case study (see Box 10.7).

Box 10.7
Competing with the Unorganised Sector

A leading brand of optical whitener (a blue powder) faced competition in the western region of India. Cheap blue powders from local manufacturers having better distribution locally were making inroads into the market and sales of the brand was falling. The loss was primarily in rural markets. Two districts were selected for testing the counter strategy to meet competition from the unorganised sector. Data was collected on all the villages in these two districts, regarding their population, number of shops and distance from nearby towns. On the basis of the above data, a van route was mapped so as to cover 52 villages having a population between 500 to 15,000, in a manner that ensured at least once a month coverage of the outlets. Promotion was directed at both the consumer and the trade. The trade promotion included quantity discounts for dealers to increase stocking and a gift scheme was introduced for small dealers. Promotion to consumers included advertising and demonstration. The advertising was through wall paintings, van paintings, window displays for exposure, dealer boards, point of purchase materials and leaflets. Education of the consumer was through demonstrations of the brand and also the other cheap blue powder. This helped to show that the cheap blue powder left a thin film of blue as particles got stuck to the pores of the cloth. This provided evidence to the consumer that the cheap blue powder had just a blue colouring effect unlike the lead brand being promoted that had a whitening effect. The result was a large increase in sales.

Ensure Dealer Returns and Prestige: In many product markets there is a segment of buyers which is quality conscious. This is more so in products where the involvement of the buyer is high, as in the purchase of high value items.

This segment is relevant for the organised sector. There is one major obstacle that such marketers face. The price attractiveness and dealer/retailer push sometimes work in tandem to persuade the consumer from this segment to buy the item of the small/unorganized sector. The margin provided by the marketer in the organised sector becomes ineffective as the retailers tend to sell the organised sector brands as loss leaders i.e., sell these brands below cost or at relatively low prices to attract customers. Some marketers have found it useful to control distribution margins and prices by limiting the number of dealers and preventing price-cutting (see Box 10.8).

Box 10.8
Ensure Dealer Return and Prestige
to Retain Channel Interest

A leading marketer of luggage products competes against very low priced luggage imitations. In small towns the unorganised sector provides dealers with hefty margins and this along with lower prices were pulling consumers away from well known brand names. The dealer sold the well known brands on very low margins and so preferred to push the unorganised sector product. The dealer gives up the relatively modest margin of the known brand in order to compete against other dealers who cut prices on that brand. In this particular market it was decided that the well known brand will be made available to consumers through only one dealer, as there was only one dealer to service that town and surrounding villages. The dealer found it sensible to push this brand as he was the only privileged seller and attracted traffic into his store. This helped not only retain the quality conscious buyer but also won over some of the undecided buyers.

Competing against Duplicates and Imitations: Leading brands very often find themselves confronted with this phenomenon in rural markets. The rising aspiration levels has encouraged fakes, especially in the case of beauty products. The face cream 'Fair and Lovely' has imitations like 'Funny and Lovely' and 'Fame and Lovely' (David, 2000). Marketers have two views on this competitive situation and take measures to counter this (see Figure 10.2). The view point dictates the response. One view point is that the segments are insulated and that the quality conscious buyer is unlikely to prefer imitations, therefore he will be careful to avoid duplicates. The argument is that imitations and duplicates help to increase the market size because of their reach and cost. The

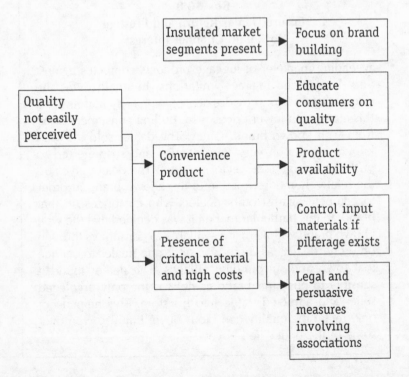

Figure 10.2 Measures to Counter Duplicates and Imitations

consumers can later upgrade to the original/genuine brand. The efforts of these brands therefore lay the foundation for brand penetration.

The strategy of letting imitations survive is suitable for high-priced quality brands and where the growth potential for quality conscious buyers exist. The second approach is to educate consumers to beware of imitations and this is suitable for products and brands where difference in quality is not easily perceived and will result in loss of market share, e.g., Virat Crane.

The second perspective requires creating awareness and knowledge among the consumers. Presumably, rural consumers are illiterate and are easily influenced. The marketer therefore needs to educate the consumer on brand quality and at the same time make the product conveniently available to him/her. In products and markets where judging quality is difficult, the approach to associate a brand with a quality image is an important method to compete against the unorganised sector. This is particularly relevant for imitations. Some marketers however, perceive a need to take additional steps over and above promotion and effective reach. They prefer to use methods to persuade, influence and increase the cost of the marketers of duplicates. The focus is on areas where scale economies are required and to plug leakages in those areas. For example, in case the packaging is not easily available then the company exercises care to see that the wrapper or packaging is not pilfered and/or available loose for outsiders. Control in packing material is exercised to avoid pilferage. Similarly, control on input material required for production negatively affects the quality of duplicate products. This quality difference is then promoted. In addition to the above, use of producer's associations to pressurise the manufacturers of duplicates to stop producing duplicates or the use of legal methods to restrain the manufacture of duplicates, is observed (see Box 10.9).

Box 10.9
P&G Initiates Raids on Brand Pirates

A research study by A.C. Neilsen indicated that the sales of Vicks look-alike products equalled the sales of the actual brand. P&G initiated action against manufacturers of look-alikes of Vicks 'vaporub' and lozenges. The company obtained an injunction from the court and then with the assistance of the court receiver's representatives and advocates, it conducted raids on the premises of Raj Remedies and seized products valued at Rs 3.5 million. These included a look-alike vaporising rub being marketed under the brand name 'Vikas', cough drops under the name 'Venus' and a menthol drop under the name 'Super Plus 5' (*The Economic Times*, October 19, 2000).

Competing with Substitutes

This is very critical in rural markets, as most leading brands compete with substitutes when they enter the market or when they launch a drive for market development. The strategy marketers use include education of key influencers in the community about the product advantages (see Box 10.10).

Box 10.10
Key Influences to Communicate Advantages and Diffuse the Product

According to Shiva Kumar, General Manager (Marketing) of HLL, 'there is the whole issue of PR, where the sarpanch, school teacher and village doctor play an important part in communicating the product's worthiness to the end user. For instance, we at HLL regard the primary health centres as one of the focal points for spreading awareness about our products' (Bamzai, 1999).

While competing with substitutes, a critical aspect is to induce trials through sampling and demonstration of product advantages, as done by HLL to demonstrate the benefits of their shampoo. The product, price and packaging is designed to induce trial (see Box 10.11).

Box 10.11
Pricing and Packaging as a Relative Advantage

- D. Shiva Kumar, General Manager, Marketing (Personal Products) of HLL says, 'All four P's apply in the hinterland, but price is the single most important determining factor. But the marketer's job is to find the right proposition, product, or solution for the rural customer. There are enough examples of product and packaging innovation that have resulted in instant successes (Brooke Bond A1, Wheel, Kissan, Annapurna, Lipton Tiger) in the rural market. The rural consumer's quantity of consumption is less as his share of wallet for these items is clearly delineated. Food and agricultural inputs dominate; whatever is left is used to fulfill aspirational needs'.

- Colgate–Palmolive has planned developing the market for its toothpowder because of its potential. Over 66 percent of rural households still use non-dentifrice products like ash, charcoal, neem sticks, salt, husk and tobacco. Following the lowering of excise duties for toothpowder, Colgate has reduced prices even further to reach a wider-cross section of people. It recently test-marketed the 50 gm. pouches of Colgate toothpowder in Andhra Pradesh and Tamil Nadu and now proposes to market the same in the northern and the eastern regions.

- Colgate toothpowder is being retailed at Rs 33.75, Rs 18.75 and Rs 9.80 for 200 gm., 150 gm., and 50 gm. cans respectively. The 10 gm. sachet is priced at Rs 1.50 and the 50 gm. pouch retails at Rs 6.00.

- Explaining the rationale for the new 50 gm. pouch, the company spokesperson said that modern dentifrices are perceived as expensive and beyond the reach of everyone in the family, 'typically, the use of modern dentifrices is restricted to only some members of the family while others use traditional or cheaper products. By offering Colgate toothpowder in more affordable pouch packs which cost 40 percent less for the same quantity, our aim is to encourage the conversion of the entire family to modern dentifrices'.

These strategies derive their conceptual basis from diffusion of innovations where the innovators and early adopters are important influences in communicating the advantages to the community. The acceptance of the product depends upon:

1. The relative advantage over the substitutes (see Box 10.12);
2. Trialability;
3. Observability;
4. Complexity; and
5. Compatibility.

Box 10.12
Consumer Perceived Relative Advantage
Hastens Diffusion

A leading petroleum company launched liquid petroleum gas (LPG) in certain rural pockets. The launch had its share of technical difficulties. One of the most important problems related to distribution. The problem was resolved using mobile filling stations. The availability of these filling stations on pre-announced days at designated spots took care of the problem of refills. The company found to their pleasant surprise that the product acceptance was high. The reason was that it replaced firewood which had a very high price/performance ratio, i.e., a very low relative advantage for firewood. The villagers had to collect firewood which was becoming scarcer by the day. This, therefore, required an adult to take time off for collecting firewood and therefore loss of wage for the day. The price to be paid for LPG, considered to be high, worked out cheaper for the villager than collecting firewood. LPG was also a much more convenient and efficient fuel. The relative advantage and the cost therefore favoured LPG. The cost for LPG was its price and firewood, the day's wage.

The applications of these concepts to new product development and launch is demonstrated in the case of the fuel wood stove, ASTRA *Ole*.

Strategise Implementation

In urban markets, promotion campaigns or the launch of products are performed on a national or regional basis. The launch can be a simultaneous one or a roll-out reaching the entire market. In the case of rural markets the sheer size of the market makes it very difficult to access, even using a roll-out plan, creating a barrier to implementation. This suggests utilisation of resources that produces effective results. A strategy to focus on villages, *haats* and *melas* to best utilise resources appears to be a viable alternative. The success of this strategy lies in the selection of villages, *haats* and *melas*.

Focus on Select Villages: IMRB study and a study by the marketing and research team suggests a correlation between the size of the village and the purchasing power of the people. Focusing distribution and promotion efforts in the 2000 plus population villages is an effective strategy according to the results of these studies. (see Box 10.13)

Box 10.13
Focus on Selective Locations

A. Launch of operation 'Super Shakti':
Colgate–Palmolive's marketing strategy' 'Super Shakti' for rural India selects villages for its promotion efforts. The strategy follows the value pouch route for toothpowder and non-conventional media (road shows, contests, sampling, posters, wall paintings and screenings of popular films). The implementation of this strategy is by the selection of two villages within a radius of five kilometers of every town for the promotional activities. (*Business India*, April 30, 2000, p. 14)

B. Selection of districts for promotional programmes:
Godrej Soaps set up an internal task force to look into the growth opportunities in rural market. The team identified ten districts spread over mainly in Andhra Pradesh and West Bengal to carry out its exercise. The team conducts van operations and wall paintings for promoting toilet soaps in these rural areas and demonstrates the company's hair dye brands. Godrej's expenditure was about Rs. ten million for this rural expansion exercise, which was to be completed by November, 1999. This exercise is important for Godrej Soaps as rural sales account for one third of its sales. (*Financial Express*, Aug 11, 1999, p. 7).

***Focus on Select* Haats:** The marketing and research team study found that the larger *haats* are generally held in bigger villages because of better road and transport connections and higher purchasing power available in the host villages—4,300 are held in the 5000+ category and another 10,300 in the 2000 to 4,999 population villages. By targeting just 14,600 distribution points, a marketer can reach almost 50 percent of the rural population, as each *haat* caters to an average of 25 villages.

***Focus on Select* Melas:** Marketers should pick *melas* close to the large villages. The list of long duration, regional and national level commercial *melas* does not exceed 500 all over India. By using the *melas* to create awareness about brands, a company can hope to reach almost half the population of rural India at a fraction of the cost as compared to other media options (Kashyap, 1998).

Support Tools for Focus in Implementation: Software packages now provide data on rural India to aid the focus on high potential locations in rural markets. Marketers can use criteria on the basis of which the software package identifies the required locations. The marketer can use criteria like male–female ratio, income levels, literacy levels, accessibility, distance from the nearest town, bank deposits, schools, dispensaries. The marketer can provide weightage for each of these dimensions and based on this the software lists all the locations. The marketer can select the areas which meet the required criteria. One of the software packages uses five criteria : demographic, literacy, agriculture, civic amenities and income. This software package can sort the entire nation and list the most suitable districts. It also lists all the villages within a district that match the requirements specified by the marketer (Rajshekar, 1999).

A Last Word

Rural markets are for marketers with persverance and creativity. The market is extremely attractive with its vast potential but also provides challenges. It is a classic case of risk–return situation. It is a high risk area but with the promise of a large customer following as the prize for those who succeed. The key to reducing the risk is to understand the market, the consumer needs and behaviour.

A marketer needs to understand that rural consumers are not a homogeneous lot. The rural market is not synonymous with the farmer. The consumer groups here differ by occupation, income, social and cultural groupings. The rural marketer will find it useful to identify consumer groups who require products purchased in the urban market. The rural market has a significant group in the service sector, either with the government or the organised sector, and this group is a ready market for urban products.

A marketer keen on tapping the potential of the rural market has to look beyond dishing out the same products that are offered in the urban market. He needs to understand the context of the product use and the behaviour of consumers. This will aid in developing and offering products that are tailored to the needs of the rural consumer, like electrical products that can withstand voltage fluctuations or rugged products that can withstand difficult conditions. This applies to both durables and non-durables like food where the product and packaging should be such that it has a long shelf life and can be preserved under different conditions. The use behaviour of the consumer is critical in designing the product, whether it is a pan holder for a stove or the chemical composition for a detergent. The marketer interested in succeeding in rural markets has to have an open mind to understand the rural consumer and a creative approach to provide a satisfactory offering.

Adaptation to consumer needs of the rural market is reflected in products offered and the message used. Understanding and communicating in the language that the rural consumer comprehends is a challenge the marketer has to face. The communication strategy that allows flexibility and autonomy to meet the local situation is important. Consumer purchase behaviour is also reflected in distribution decisions. The periodic markets are an important social institution that marketers can use to supplement reaching the rural consumer.

Competition in rural markets is different from urban markets; from the small and unorganised sector and imitations it is strengthened by low literacy and awareness levels of rural consumers. The marketer has to also compete with substitutes. This requires education on the product unlike brand promotion in urban markets. The three C's critical in rural markets are the consumers, channels and competition. The variations in these result in a large number of combinations. To add to this complexity is the widespread rural market. Clearly, for the enterprising entrant there is a combination waiting to be exploited, and so plenty of room in the market. The tenacious veteran brand with its hold on the channel is there to sustain loyalty and market share. There is however no dearth of opportunity for creative marketing in the exciting arena of rural markets.

Decision Implications

The implications for a marketer is influenced by the type of competitive situation and the challenge presented by the rural markets.

Competitive Situation and Strategic Response:
The key to developing a strategy is an understanding of the competitive situation by the marketer. The marketer who introduces a new brand has to invest in promoting the brand position and support it with distribution efforts. It is critical to get the brand to the shelf of the village shop. The marketer not having the strength in distribution will find it useful to enter into an alliance for access. Marketers of durables can explore a tie-up with small manufacturers or those in the unorganised sector for taking up dealership. This is important for durables that require frequent servicing.

Retention of share with the entry of new brands is a growing challenge even in rural markets. Quality products that meet the needs of buyers and satisfy them is important even for non-durables as word-of-mouth is important in rural markets. Effective servicing of channels is an important line of defence, as stockouts are a route to enter the rural markets. The problem of retention is acute when faced with competition from the unorganised sector. One option for an existing brand is to focus on the quality conscious buyer and intensify distribution and promotion through the classic route of vans. The use of exclusive dealers to support the effort is also required. The second more aggressive option is to compete in the larger mass market. The introduction of lower priced brands, small package size and demonstration of quality compared to the competition makes use of the 'value for money' proposition.

Competing with duplicates and imitations require a different approach depending on the situation. Where evidence of superior quality of the brand can be demonstrated to the consumers, the focus is to be on brand building. In case of products where product performance is not evident, education on need for quality and promoting image of quality is important. An approach used in many situations is to increase the cost of operation of duplicates and imitations to make it unviable. This can be through the control of critical input materials or through creation of legal hurdles.

The rural marketer frequently has to compete with substitutes, whether the product is shampoo, toothpaste or a washing machine. In competing with substitutes, the marketer can increase consumer acceptance by:

– education using demonstration, and
– designing a product with relative superiority which can be easily perceived by the rural consumer

Implementation of distribution and promotion decisions are a critical challenge for the marketer. In rural markets therefore, there is a need to reach the markets through multiple channels; retail, *haats* and *melas*. The positioning efforts in the rural markets including the *haats* and *melas* need to use methods that compel the attention of the audience, like games and demonstration. In addition to the above, the efficient use of resources to launch campaigns suggests a focus on select villages, *haats* and *melas*. The distribution and promotion should be targeted to reach villages with a 2000 plus population, *haats* held in these villages and 500 of the commercial *melas* which are of long duration. This approach will effectively and efficiently reach a large percentage of the rural population.

References

Bamzai, Sandeep, 'Marketers now target Bharat', *Business India*, September 6–17, 1999.

David, Robin, 'T.V. Transforming Rural India: Study', *The Times of India*, February 13, 2000.

Ganguly, Dibeyendu, 'Rasna flows straight into rural heart to boost SDC', *The Economic Times*, April 16, 2001.

Iyer, K. Sriram, 'Henkel to Charm Rural India via economy packs', *The Economic Times*, September 28, 2000.

Kala Vijayraghavan and Anamika Rath, 'FMCGs find rural treasure hunt tough', *The Economic Times*, December 15, 2000.

Kashyap, Pradeep, 'Selling to the Sons of the Soil', *Strategic Marketing*, Vol. I, No. 4, August–October, 1998.

Mukherjee, Biman, 'The Fairground as Battlefield', *Business Today*, December 7–21, 1993.

Rajshekar, M, 'Quest for the Rural Rest', *A&M*, March 31, 1999.

The Economic Times, 'Colgate-Palmolive to make oral care accessible in rural areas', April 5, 2000.

Velayudhan, Sanal Kumar and Suri, B., 'Rural Market Response—A Tentative Study', *Management and Labour Studies,* Vol. 21, No. 1, 1996.

Zaheer, Kamil, 'HLL toothpastes see glow in rural India', *The Economic Times,* August 25, 1999.

Bibliography

1. Ahmed, Shamim, (1991), 'Rural Marketing in India', Ashish Publishing House, New Delhi.

2. Amte, V.K., (1982), 'Marketing Costs and the Developing World' in Madhav, P., Kacker (ed), Marketing and Economic Development, Deep and Deep Publications, New Delhi, pp. 215-240.

3. Aneja, Rajendra, K. (1992), 'Evolving Optimum Media-Mix and Communication Strategies for Rural Markets', *Economic and Political Weekly*, May p. M-75.

4. Arathoon, Marion, (1999), 'It's the same world after all', *Brand Equity*, October 6–12.

5. Baig, M.A., (1980), 'Guidelines for Urban and Rural Marketing', *Indian Journal of Marketing*, Vol. 10, No. 5, Jan. pp. 3–8.

6. Balakrishna, M., (1977), 'Rural Market : End of a Lone Road for the Consumer Marketers?' *Decision*.

7. Bamzai, Sandeep, (1999), 'Marketers now target Bharat', *Business India*, September 6–17.

8. Baptist, Vinod, (1992), 'Promotion by Channel Members in Rural Markets'. An unpublished report submitted as part of PGDBM course, XLRI, Jamshedpur.

9. Bijapurkar, R. and Ravi Murthy, (1999), 'Rural Markets for Consumer Durables', *The Economic Times*, August 16.

10. Bose, D.K., (1992), 'Reaching out to the Rural Millions', *Brand Equity*, October 28.

11. *Business World*, (1999), 'The Undiscovered Country', April 7–12.

12. Chandra, Prafulla, T.V., (1992), 'Communicating Health Information to Rural People', *Kurukshetra*, February.

13. Chatterjee, Adite, (1992), 'Marketers Hit the Rural Dirt Trucks', *Brand Equity*, October 24.

14. Chatterjee, Adite, Asha Rai and Nandini Lakshman, (1992), 'Gambling on the Rural Roulette', *Brand Equity*, April 8.

15. Chokalingham, G., (1990), 'Reaping the Rural Reward', *Brand Equity*, October 30.

16. Das Gupta, Surajeet and Ramesh Menon, (1990), 'Rural Markets: The Call of Consumerism' *India Today*, July 15.

17. Das, Sandeep, (1994), 'Advertising in Rural Markets: Message Effectiveness'. An unpublished report submitted as part of PGDBM course, XLRI, Jamshedpur.

18. Das, V. Mukunda, (1982), 'Some Aspects of Rural Markets in India', *The Economic Times*, May 26–27.

19. David, Robin, (2000), 'MICA Market Rating Could Save Many A Product', *The Times of India*, February 13.

20. Dhawan, Paulomi, (1996), 'The Monolith Stars', *A&M*, April 15.

21. Dhawan, Paulomi, (1998), 'Marketing Ammo', *A&M*, May 1–15.

22. Dhillon, G., (1980), 'Rural Women in Decision Making—A Study', *Kurukshetra*, Vol. 28, No. 9, February 1, pp. 19–21.

23. 'Distribution of Consumer Articles in Rural Areas through Co-operatives—Some Problems', 1979, *The Co-operator*, Vol. 17, No. 11, December, pp. 353–354.

24. Doshi, H.N., (1972), 'Promotion and Advertising in Rural Marketing', in *New Opportunities in Changing Agriculture*, Ahmedabad; CMA (IIMA), pp. 141–150.

25. Gaikwad, V.K., (1972), 'A Search for the Rural Consumer', in *New Opportunities in Changing Agriculture*, Ahmedabad; CMA (IIMA), pp. 159–172.

26. Gairola, Manoj, (2000), 'Inmarsat to Set Up Satellite Telephones in Rural Areas', *The Economic Times*, November 17.

27. George, P.S., (1972), 'Development of Rural Markets in India', *Indian Journal of Marketing*, Vol. 2, No. 5, January, pp. 9–11.

28. Ghosh, Aparisim, (1994), 'The New Rules of Rural Marketing', *Business World*, April 6–19.

29. Ghosh, Joydeep and Chetan Krishnaswamy, (1997), 'The Rural Rush', *The Week*, Vol. 15, No. 44.

30. Gore, Mrinal, (1979), 'The Rural Consumer: An Unprotected Lot', *Vikalpa*, Vol. 4, No. 3, July, pp. 245–248.

31. Goyal. (1986), 'Buyer Behaviour of Tractor Owners', *Indian Journal of Marketing*, Vol. 16, No. 10.

32. Das Gupta, Surajeet and Ramesh Menon, (1990), 'Rural Markets; The Call of Consumerism', *India Today*, July 15.

33. Gupta, V.K., (1972), 'An Approach to Rural Marketing', *Indian Journal of Marketing*, Vol. 2, No. 5, January, pp. 12–20.

34. ICICI, (1979), 'Rural Marketing : A Pilot Study', Mumbai.

35. Iyer, Sriram, K., (2000), 'Henkel to Charm Rural India via Economy Packs', *The Economic Times*, September 28.

36. Jha, Mithleshwar, (1999), 'Rural Marketing: Some Conceptual Issues', *Rural Scan*, Vol. 1, No. 2, April.

37. Joshi, Anjali, (1991), 'Rural Markets: The New El Dorado', *The Sunday Observer*, April 28–May 4.

38. Kacker, B. and P. Kacher, (1979), 'Cultural Considerations in Researching the Rural Markets—A Note', *Decision*, Vol. 6 No. 4, October, pp. 439–442.

39. Kala, Vijayraghavan and Rath Anamika (2000), 'FMCGs Find Rural Treasure Hunt Tough', *The Economic Times*, December 15.

40. Kapoor, M.C., (1976), 'Profile of a Rural Consumer—A Study', *Indian Management*, Vol. 15, No. 11, November, pp. 7–11.

41. Kashyap, Pradeep, (2000), 'Rural People Look up to Urbanites', *A&M*, January 15.

42. Kashyap, Pradeep, (1998), 'Selling to the Sons of the Soil', *Strategic Marketing*, Vol. 1, No. 4, August–October.

43. Kilaru, Sudheer, (1994), 'Study of Retailer Behaviour in Rural Market', an unpublished report prepared as part of PGDBM course at XLRI, Jamshedpur.

44. Kohok, M.A., (1973), 'Marketing for 123 Million Rural Consumers', *Indian Journal of Commerce*, Vol. 26, No. 4, November, pp. 716–722.

45. Krishna, M., (1974), 'Rural Markets Coverage by Mail Order', *Indian Journal of Marketing*, Vol. 6, No. 1–2, pp. 12–13.

46. Krishnamurthy, Narayan, (1999), 'Signs Speak Louder', *A&M*, November 30.

47. Kulshreshtha, Rajal, (1998), 'Regional Round-Up', *A&M*, May 1–15.

48. Lahiri, Sanat, (1971), 'Evolving an Effective Strategy for Tapping the Rural Markets', *Capital*, July 22, pp. 24–28.

49. Law, Vivek, (2000), 'Rural India Rings a Bell for Mobile Majors', *The Economic Times*, December 21.

50. Mathew, M.O. and S. Sudalaimathu, (1980), 'Consumer Motivation with Reference to Rural Industries Products', *Indian Journal of Marketing*, Vol. XI, No. 3, November, p. 9.

51. Mathur, Navin, (1981), 'Rural Marketing', *Indian Journal of Marketing*, Vol. 2, No. 8, April, pp. 3–8.

52. Mathur, V.B.L., (1979), 'Serving the Rural Consumer', *The Cooperator*, Vol. 17, No. 4, August 15, pp. 77–78.

53. Mehta, Mona, (2001), 'Rural Push: Sansui Sets Aside Rs. 40 crore Adspend Till 2002', *The Financial Express*, January 17.

54. Mehta, A.D., (1985), 'Rural Market Centres', *The Economic Times*, January 9–10.

55. Mehta, S.C., (1973), 'Survey of Rural Tamil Nadu: Consumer Durables—Poor Penetration in Villages', *The Economic Times*, July 1, pp. 4–6.

56. Michael, U.P., (1979), 'Determinants of Consumer Behaviour in a Rural Based Retail Market—An Empirical Study of Foot-Wear Market in Kolhapur', *Decision*, Vol. 6, No. 2, April, pp. 175–186.

57. Misra, Shefali, (1992), 'Floating on Idea'. *Strategist*, August 4.

58. Misra, Shefali, (1992), 'The Forbidden Land'. *Strategist*, December 1.

59. Mohan, M., (1979), 'Marketing in Rural India', *Productivity*, Vol. XIX, No. 4, January–March, pp. 619–631.

60. Monga, J.S., (1972), 'Rural Marketing: Planning and Strategy,' *Indian Journal of Marketing*, Vol. 2, No. 5, January, pp. 4–9.

61. Mukherjee, Biman, (1993), 'The Fairground as Battlefield', *Business Today*, December 7–12.

62. Mukund, Das, and Somnath, Sen, (1991), 'Commercial Aspect: The Rural Way', *A&M* October.

63. *The Economic Times*, Mumbai Bureau, (1999), 'Buoyant Rural Demand Takes Hind Lever Q2 net up 25%', July 26.

64. Nag, Ashoke, (2000), 'Star TV moves to woo rural India', *The Economic Times*, October 2.

65. National Council of Applied Economic Research, (NCAER), (1998), 'India Market Demographics Report 1998', New Delhi.

66. Ogilvy & Mather Media, (1996), 'Rural Media Web Untangled', *Brand Equity*, May 8–14.

67. Pandit, S., (1972), 'Marketing of Consumer Goods in Rural Areas', in *New Opportunities in Changing Agriculture*, Ahmedabad: CMA (IIMA), pp. 151–156.

68. Paul, E.J., (1972), 'The Role of Advertising in the Emerging Rural Markets', in *New Opportunities in Changing Agriculture*, Ahmedabad: CMA (IIMA), pp. 173–182.

69. Pawan, Bhandari, and Rajat, Iyer, (1995), 'Getting your message across' *A&M*, February 15.

70. Puri, S., (1971), 'Rural Families and Decision Making Pattern, *Indian Journal of Extension Education*, Vol. 7, No. 1–2, March–June, pp. 65–69.

71. Rai, Asha, (2000), 'Titan Chimes Rural Tunes with Sonata', *The Economic Times*, August 18.

72. Rajan, R.V., (1999), 'Marketing a Go-Go', *Brand Equity*, September 29–October 5.

73. Rajan, R.V., (1999), 'Village Flair', *Brand Equity*, September 29–October 5.

74. Rajan, Ravi, (1992), 'Changing the role of the devil', *Brand Equity*, October 28.

75. Rajan, Ravi, (1992), 'Hooking on to a New Channel', *Brand Equity*, August 12.

76. Rajendran, Vasanthi, (1992), 'Traditional Media as Agents of Change', *Vidura*, Vol. 28, No. 2, March–April, p. 45.

77. Rajshekar, M., (1999), 'Quest for the Rural Rest', *A&M*, March 31.

78. Ramaswamy, V.S., (1972), 'Mass Communication for Rural Marketing', *Indian Journal of Marketing*, Vol. 2, No. 5, January, pp. 26–31.

79. Rao, Narsimha G.V.L., (1992), 'Creating Markets in the Country Side', *Brand Equity*, November 18.

80. Rao, S. L., (1973), 'Rural Marketing of Consumer Goods', *Economic and Political Weekly*, Vol. 8, No. 34, August 25, M 77–79.

81. Rao, K.G.K. and R.G. Tagat, (1985), 'Rural Marketing: A Developmental Approach', *Vikalpa*, 10, 3, July–September, pp. 315–326.

82. Ray, Siddhartha, (1998), 'A Bird's Eye View', *A&M*, May 1–15.

83. Saini, D.R., (1972), 'Strategy for Rural Marketing, Vol. 2, No. 5, January, pp. 22–25.

84. Salil, Saras, (1998), 'Going for the Numbers', *A&M*, June 30.

85. Velayudhan, Sanal Kumar and Suri, B., (1996), 'Rural Market Response—A Tentative Study', *Management and Labour Studies*, Vol. 21, No. 1.

86. Velayudhan, Sanal Kumar, (1995), 'Urban Reference and Divided Rural Market: Search for a Framework', *Indian Journal of Marketing*, Vol. 24, No. 4.

87. Velayudhan, Sanal Kumar, (1994), 'Rural Markets: Transition and Issues', paper presented at the Sixth Annual Management Education Convention of the Association of Indian Management School, August.

88. Velayudhan, Sanal Kumar, (1998), 'Buyer Behaviour in Rural Markets: A Study of Soap Market', *Productivity*, Vol. 39, No. 2, July–September.

89. Sarkar, Bashab, (1998), 'Other side of the Coin', *A&M*, May 1–15.

90. Sarma, M.T.R. and T.R. Rao, (1981), 'Problems of Rural Marketing in India', in *New Perspectives in Marketing*, 12 (2 and 3), pp. 18–23.

91. Shirali, Aresh, (1993), 'A Matter of Perceptions', *A&M*, February.

92. Singh, Rakesh, (1998), 'A Rural Myth', *Brand Equity*, October 28–November 3.

93. Sirbhaiya, Anupam, (1994), 'The Role of Mass Media and Interpersonal Communication as a Source of Information for the Rural Consumer', an unpublished report submitted as part of PGDBM course, XLRI, Jamshedpur.

94. Social and Research Institute, (1990), 'Villages of India', A Study of Indian Market Research Bureau.

95. *The Economic Times*, Calcutta Bureau, (2000), 'Colgate–Palmolive to make Oral Care Accessible in Rural Areas', April 5.

96. Wanamali, Sudhir, (1981), 'Periodic Markets and Rural Development in India', B.R. Publishing Corporation, New Delhi.

97. Yadava, J.S., (1972), 'Communication Patterns and New Consumers in Rural India', in *New Opportunities in Changing Agriculture*, Ahmedabad, CMA (IIMA), pp. 183–194.

98. Zaheer, Kamil, (1999), 'HLL toothpastes see glow in Rural India', *The Economic Times*, August 25.